NO PART TO PLAY

MAURIZIO CUCCHI

MAURIZIO CUCCHI

No Part to Play

Selected Poems 1965–2009

Handwritten inscription:
APRIL 19, 2021

FOR JOHN AND KAY,

IN HOPES OF SEEING
YOU BOTH AGAIN
SOON,

AS EVER,
Michael

Translated by ~~Michael Palma~~ .

 Chelsea Editions

Chelsea Editions, a press of Chelsea Associates, Inc., a not-for-profit corporation under section 501 (c) (3) of the United States Internal Revenue Code, has the support of the Sonia Raiziss Giop Charitable Foundation.

Italian text taken from *Poesie 1965–2000*, *Per un secondo o un secolo*, and *Vite pulviscolari*, all written by Maurizio Cucchi and published by Arnoldo Mondadori Editore S.p.A., Milano. And reprinted here with the gracious permission of the aforementioned publishers. Italian text copyright © 2001, 2003, 2009 by Arnoldo Mondadori Editore S.p.A., Milano.

Translation © 2013 by Michael Palma
Introduction © 2013 by Michael Palma

Author photo by Valeria Poggi
Cover photo by Maurizio Cucchi
Book design by Lisa Cicchetti

Library of Congress Cataloging-in-Publication Data

Maurizio Cucchi, 1945
No Part to Play: Selected Poems 1965–2009
Selected, edited, and introduced by Michael Palma
Maurizio Cucchi, translated by Michael Palma, p. 288

ISBN 978-0-9884787-3-2
1. Cucchi, Maurizio—Translation into English
2. Palma, Michael, 1945– II. Title

Manufactured in the United States of America by Thomson-Shore, Inc.

First Edition 2013

Chelsea Editions
Box 125, Cooper Station
New York, NY 10276-0125

www.chelseaeditionsbooks.org

For Luigi Bonaffini,
fratello nell'arte

—M. P.

CONTENTS

Introduction

"Whatever it is," wrote Louis Simpson about American poetry more than half a century ago, "it must have / A stomach that can digest / Rubber, coal, uranium, moons, poems." From Whitman on, there have been many American poets of flexible art and comprehensive vision to fit Simpson's specifications. But we tend, rightly or wrongly, to think of other poets, especially European ones, as less omnivorous than our own, more focused in their thematic concerns and more conscious of their classical inheritance. For these reasons, and others, American readers should find themselves readily responsive to the poetry of Maurizio Cucchi, despite what might be described as its inherent strangeness. (In calling his poetry strange, I don't in the least mean to be pejorative, since strangeness is a defining characteristic of much of the greatest literature: writing with no trace of the strange is safe and bland; and what, after all, could be weirder than the *Inferno*?) Cucchi's poetry is marked to an unusual degree by intellectual curiosity and a wide range of concerns, giving it a depth and a richness of interest missing from the work of a great many other poets. It contains and integrates, often in the same poem, the items in Simpson's list and a great many others—gritty urban landscapes and somewhat less cluttered rural ones; frequent references to sports (soccer and especially competitive cycling) and athletes; allusions to great works of European and American literature, and to historical figures and events. His interest in the world around him has kept pace with the world itself: in one recent poem, he makes extensive use of technical terminology to draw a witty comparison between the speaker's brain and the workings of a computer.

Much of the time, such notations of the outside world alternate with—or speak through, or serve as masks for—personal details and reminiscences. These include recollections of his childhood and Catholic upbringing, early relationships, descriptions of his beloved Milan (where he has lived his entire life and which is also the subject of his 2007 volume of prose sketches, *La traversata di Milano*), and details of his travels in Europe and Africa. In the process, Cucchi has projected a sense of the individual personality as fluid and even unstable, existing in a dynamic tension between what is within and outside of itself. In describing the arc of his career to that point, Alba Donati offers this analysis in her critical essay appended to Cucchi's comprehensive collection, *Poesie 1965–2000*: "Now, with the publication of *Glenn's Last*

Journey [1999], we can come to terms with a long and complex journey which has modified its modes and tones, clarifying them, but which has confirmed what was already present at the source. . . . Cucchi's poetry posed and poses the problem of the friction between autobiography and impersonality; between concealment and exposure; between lyrical writing and narrative modes; between realism and oneiric vision; between a renunciative and nihilistic inclination and a positive and ethical vocation; between, better still, a private and solitary numbness and an epical determination for ordinary life."

One of Cucchi's most significant themes involves his feelings about and relationships with his parents, especially his father. Threaded through the body of his poetry is the central, shattering fact of the young Cucchi's existence, the disappearance and death of his adored father, Luigi, which occurred in May 1957, when the boy was not yet twelve years old. He was plunged into an atmosphere of mystery and confusion which was not resolved for nearly four decades until his mother told him in 1996 how anxiety over business reverses and mounting debts had led his father to take his own life. The title of Cucchi's first book of poems, *The Missing* (*Il disperso*, 1976), makes an oblique reference to his father's disappearance, and it is also the subject of the first major poem in the collection, "The House, the Outsiders, the Near Relations." While Cucchi has justifiably objected to those who overstate the significance of this element in his work, that father is nonetheless the animating figure of a number of poems, among them some of Cucchi's finest: "Letter and Prayer," "Glenn's Journey," "'53," and especially "Glenn's Last Journey."

Despite the preoccupation with very personal and at times deeply painful experience, Cucchi's poetry is notable for its even tone, its avoidance of stylistic excess and rhetorical extravagance. He uses fewer exclamation points than almost any other poet. His diction is straightforward, with frequent flavorings of technical and colloquial terms. While there is very little rhyme in his work, there is everywhere a strong underpinning of traditional metrics, particularly the hendecasyllabic, enriched by frequent alliteration and other sound values. Though there are periodic flashes of irony and some acerbic descriptions, especially of people, his chief vehicle of communication is the image, precisely etched and seemingly neutral in presentation. His preference is to let descriptions, and their juxtapositions, speak for themselves, without preaching or hectoring, without pointing a moral or adorning a tale. When, as in "Money and Things," he engages the subject of the materialism of modern culture, he does so not from a standpoint of facile moral superiority, but with full complicity in the situations he describes. In this he is reminiscent of the refreshing attitude toward his fellow humans expressed by Bertolt Brecht (in Michael Hamburger's translation): "I say: they are animals with a quite peculiar smell / And I say: does it matter? I am too."

In combining these elements in just this way, Cucchi has, it seems to me, struck an original note in contemporary poetry. Originality, which barely existed as a literary desideratum until about two hundred years ago, is a highly prized concept in our present-day artistic culture. For many, "new" is a necessary—and for some, it seems, the only—criterion of merit. Yet, as overused as the term may be, there are instances in which it properly applies, and here, I believe, is one such instance. There are of course points of contact between Cucchi's work and that of other poets. As someone once suggested, there is no such thing as true originality, since anything we can imagine is simply a recombination of familiar elements in a different way. So, like others before him, Cucchi has combined familiar things in an unfamiliar way, and has thus created a poetry that is wholly and unmistakably his own.

In an interview with Giovanna Frene published in the Spring 2006 issue of *Gradiva*, Cucchi was asked about the influence of Eliot and Pound on his poetry, and he responded in part: "Regarding Eliot's work, *Prufrock and Other Observations* was the thing I preferred by far—even though I greatly valued *The Waste Land* and *Four Quartets* . . .—because it is also 'didactic,' in the sense that it makes you understand what can be contained in poetry, namely anything: then it depends on each individual's ear, on the capacity to absorb the materials, on the speech below the surface." It is not surprising that he should be most drawn to Eliot's earliest work, in that, as I have said elsewhere, Cucchi's "sensibility is decidedly secular." Yet a case can also be made for the influence of *The Waste Land* on his poetry. Here I'm thinking principally—though by no means exclusively—of "Glenn's Last Journey," the title piece of a chapbook he published in 1998; it is his ultimate and most definitive attempt to come to terms with his father's death, and it remains one of his finest accomplishments. It has been asserted that, despite *The Waste Land*'s purported immense influence on modern poetry, there is no other poem that even remotely resembles it; this may have been true at one time, and for a long time, but I would maintain that there are a number of significant similarities to be noted between Eliot's poem and Cucchi's. They include such previously mentioned characteristics as historical references, literary allusions and quotations, and the intermingling of these elements with disturbing personal experiences. Another central point of contact is each poet's procedure through an accretion of fragments, creating a kaleido-scope of scenes and incidents and a medley of shifting voices.

The shoring of fragments into longer poems and sequences is a struc-tural technique that Cucchi has employed throughout his career, a hallmark of his work. In his earlier collections he tended to group these components into numbered sections; thereafter, his practice has been to separate them with rows of asterisks. Especially in his later work, this approach has often involved the combining of disparate and seemingly unrelated materials, with abrupt shifts of speaker, tone, and subject matter (yet, paradoxically, even as he has grown more oblique in some respects, he has also become less so in others: like many another poet, he has, as a general tendency, grown less elliptical, more discursive over time). Though these individual components are usually seen as detachable, with Cucchi often represented in anthologies by excerpted sections and stanzas, I have decided to include in this volume only poems and sequences translated in their entirety. This approach has forced me to omit many fine isolated passages from elsewhere in the body of his work, but I chose to preserve the integrity of the chosen texts and to allow their internal relationships to present themselves.

In the *Gradiva* interview, Cucchi goes on to say: "At the same time I was greatly attracted by the most extremist elements of Pound; it was also the period of Pop Art, and Pound's 'picking up and putting in' interested me very much (and still does); in fact it's the process on which I based *Il disperso* in particular: the estrangement, also the taking of linguistic elements, ways of speaking, other expressions (from fiction, ordinary speech, the theater, film) and moving them into another sphere: clearly the displacement creates an opening of meaning and a sequence of virtuality. In any case, the spoken word, the orality, was one of the things that interested me most: taking frag-ments of actual speech and inserting them into poetry."

It is worth noting that Cucchi has applied this lesson with much greater consistency of effect than does his source and inspiration; as Karl Shapiro remarked more than half a century ago, "Pound has never really stopped being archaic . . . and even in the late *Cantos* when he becomes moved he drops back into the *thee's* and *thou's* and *hadst's* of old." Cucchi's diction may be what some would call impure, in its occasional mixing of levels and modes of expression, but his choices, in both language and form, are always logical and coherent. And perpetually relevant: as I write, in the current issue of *The New Republic* the critic Jed Perls quotes Albert C. Barnes's *The Art in Painting* (1925) to the effect that unity "is satisfactory only when it embraces a diversity. . . . Coherence, in brief, means not mere sameness but sameness in difference; not the unity of grains of sand but of parts of an organism which complement each other but are not all cast in the same mold."

Cucchi has learned from great masters, and he has applied their lessons with a transforming infusion of his own personality and concerns. In doing so, he has made himself into one of the last, if not the very last, of the great Modernists.

MICHAEL PALMA

da IL DISPERSO (1976)

from THE MISSING (1976)

. . . .

Certo non solo la cartella
piantata lì, appoggiata all'angolo,
allo zoccolo. Sgonfia a metà, coi manici
in disordine. Ma lui stesso, l'artefice,
supino (riverso) la bocca spalancata,
i piedi incrociati sulla sedia, gli occhiali
in terra, rotti . . .

. . . .

. . . .

Of course not only the briefcase
left there, propped up in the corner,
against the baseboard. It sags in the middle, handles
askew. But him too, the author,
on his back (turned around) mouth wide open,
his feet crossed on the chair, his glasses
on the floor, broken . . .

. . . .

La casa, gli estranei, i parenti prossimi

1

Nei pressi di . . . trovata la Lambretta. Impolverata,
a pezzi. Nessuno di noi ha mai pensato
seriamente a ritirarla. Forse la paura. Rovistando
nel cassetto, al solito, il furbo di cui al seguito
ha ripescato una fascia elastica, una foto o due,
un dente di latte e un ricciolo rimasti nel portafogli,
dieci lire (che non c'entravano per niente . . .)

In aggiunta a tutto ricordo che quando venivo su dalle scale io
era di giovedì, finita la scuola, verso mezzogiorno; ma era
anche un ritorno diverso dal solito . . . Ci sarà
un aggancio.

Adesso comunque, eccomi qui e:
— Credimi, fai caso
a quel tale andare tirandosi dietro le gambe e tutto, con gli occhietti
ancora appiccicati, nel pigiama, goffo da cane,
rigido inamidato. Ma il bello è
che me ne accorgo. E allora con che faccia
fingere un'altra volta il tono giusto, le parole,
cioè, un po' stiracchiate; il vestire in qualche modo?

The House, the Outsiders, the Near Relations

1

The Lambretta found in the area of . . . Covered with dust,
in pieces. None of us ever seriously considered
going back to fetch it. Maybe out of fear. Rummaging
in the drawer, as usual, the smart aleck (about whom more to come)
fished out a rubber band, a photo or two,
a baby tooth and a lock of curly hair in a wallet,
ten lire (which had nothing to do with it at all . . .)

In addition to everything else I remember that when I came up
     the stairs
it was Thursday, after school, around noon; but it was also
a different way back than usual . . . There might be
a connection.

Now, anyhow, here I am and:
—Trust me, pay attention
to that one trailing legs and all, with his little eyes
still glued shut, in pajamas, dog-clumsy,
stiff and starchy. But the best part is
that I realize it. And so with what face
to feign the right tone once again, the words,
that is, a little forced; dressed in some way?

(Che i morti siano due? Ma quello giusto?
Indifferente? E il primo,
come una specie di confidenza notturna, non è un parente stretto?
Strettissimo?)

(Dimmi tu se è possibile. Pochi giorni fa
era lì che faceva i suoi lavori. Pareva pacifico.)

È morto per un infarto (o per un incidente stradale, per un
    malore, per via di un sasso): sì va bene, ma ci sarà
pure un colpevole, un responsabile
diretto, qualcuno che l'ha fatto fuori.

2

Non ci voleva quel bicchiere rotto.
Poco meno di un simbolo. Poco più
di una fissazione. O viceversa. E poi
la ferita, lo zampillo, l'incerottamento. Mi spiace confessarlo,
ma per fortuna che non c'ero.

Diamo un'occhiata alla TOPOGRAFIA DELLA CASA:

— Tutte le cose, a loro modo,
erano in ordine, al posto giusto. Un senso,
capisci, non mancava. Ma quel tale
entrato poco dopo (forse, mi hai detto
dietro la tenda, uno della polizia) cos'ha capito?
Intendo del pestacarne abbandonato
sopra il frigorifero, o della mela
mezza sbucciata, tagliata, diventata nera; della bottiglia
del vermut rimasta senza tappo, in un angolo del tavolo,
col bicchiere lì . . .

(Could there be two of them dead? But the right one?
Immaterial? And the first one,
like a kind of nocturnal confidence, isn't he a close relative?
Extremely close?)

(You tell me if it's possible. A few days ago
he was right there at his job. He seemed peaceful.)

He died of a heart attack (or an accident on the road, or an
      illness, or because of a stone); yes, all right, and yet
there may still be a guilty party, someone directly
responsible, someone who got rid of him.

2

There wasn't any need for that broken glass.
A little less than a symbol. A little more
than a fixation. Or vice versa. And then
the wound, the spurt, the bandaging. It really pains me to admit it,
but luckily I wasn't there.

Let's look at the TOPOGRAPHY OF THE HOUSE:

—Everything, in its own way,
was in order, in its proper place. It had,
you understand, a certain feeling. But that one
who came in a little later (maybe, you told me
behind the curtain, one of the police) what did he understand?
I mean about the meat mallet forgotten
on top of the refrigerator, or the apple
half-peeled and sliced, that had turned black; or the bottle
of vermouth left uncapped, on the corner of the table,
with the glass there . . .

Di fuori c'erano i fiaschi, le bottiglie vuote. Tutti gli ombrelli
appesi alla sbarra di ferro della porta interna.

(C'entra qualcosa il vicino
del piano di sotto, che esce sempre dopo le undici di sera
con una faccia da vampiro?)

(Non avevo mai nascosto certe mie debolezze:
— Dal dentista,
andarci all'ora del tramonto può essere invitante.
E in più, dopo, uscire, fare il giro della casa,
tenerti la bocca, dire al primo che incontri e ti saluta: « Sai,
devi scusarmi se parlo male, o mostro un riso macabro. Ma vedi,
mi mancano i denti, proprio qui davanti . . . »

Così, dopo l'accaduto, la vicina del dentista: « Se la gente caro lei
ci pensasse un po' più spesso
ci sarebbe meno cattiveria. » E io
rosso di colpa, mezzo scemo, coi capelli
già quasi tagliati a zero
a giustificarmi come segue: « Ma io non c'entro,
io non ho fatto niente . . . l'infarto . . . lo sa bene . . . »
E mi toccavo i bottoni della giacca.)

Outside were the jugs, the empty bottles. All the umbrellas
hung up on the iron bar of the inside door.

(Does he have something to do with it,
the downstairs neighbor, who always goes out after eleven at night
with the face of a vampire?)

(I've never hidden certain of my weaknesses:
—It can be very
appealing to go to the dentist at the twilight hour.
And moreover, later, leaving, going around the house,
holding your mouth, telling the first one you meet who speaks to
        you: "You know,
you'll have to excuse me if I sound funny or have a hideous smile.
        But you see,
I'm missing some teeth, right here in the front . . ."

Thus, after the event, the dentist's neighbor: "My dear sir, if people
thought about it a little bit more
there'd be less evil in the world." And I
red with guilt, half-witted, with my hair
already cut to nearly nothing
excusing myself as follows: "But I've got nothing to do with it,
I haven't done anything . . . heart attack . . . you know . . ."
And I fiddled with the buttons of my jacket.)

3

I primi segni a ben vedere
non erano mancati. È la ricomparsa
che nessuno si poteva attendere. Dato che poi,
sulla poltrona, magari in lacrime, se ne era parlato
della sparizione. Ma in concreto, quanto ne sapevamo?

Ricordati, però, senza cercare colpe, dell'acqua
entrata di notte sotto i vetri in nostra assenza, della crepa
che taglia tutto il soffitto, addirittura del solaio
sopra la stanza in fondo e che neppure ci siamo curati di visitare,
del lampadario che dondola, degli infissi mezzi marci.

Oggi, poi, come non bastasse, guarda qui! Avvicinati,
guarda un po' qui, ti dico, qui sotto. Mi cresce la muffa,
la muffa sulla suola!

È che mio padre sì
sapeva di lettere, cultura: London,
Steinbeck, Coppi e Bartali, Oscar
Carboni e la Gazzetta
dello Sport. L'officina. E quelle camicie d'allora,
larghe, i pantaloni alti in vita, paletò palandrane . . .

Mi sono domandato il perché
di questo continuo andarsene
di inquilini, qui dell'interno. E di operai
che vanno e vengono e sporcano le scale. (Chissà adesso
come sarebbe tutta consunta la targhetta della porta.)

3

In hindsight, the first signs
weren't lacking. It's the recurrence
that no one could have expected. Given that, then,
in the armchair, maybe in tears, the disappearance was
discussed. But in reality, how much did we know about it?

You remember, however, without looking to cast blame, the water
that came in at night under the windows while we were gone, the
crack
cutting across the whole ceiling, even in the attic
over the room at the end we haven't even taken the trouble to
inspect,
the swaying chandelier, the half-rotted casings.

Today, then, as if that weren't enough, look here! Come close,
look around a bit here, I tell you, here underneath. Mould is
spreading,
mould on my soles!

It's that my father was so well
acquainted with books and culture: London,
Steinbeck, Coppi and Bartali, Oscar
Carboni and *The Sports
Gazzette*. The workshop. And the shirts from that time,
wide, pants high in the waist, overlong overcoats.

I've asked myself the reason
for tenants continually moving
out of this apartment. And for workmen
coming and going and dirtying the stairs. (Who knows
how completely worn away the nameplate on the door is now.)

4

Avevo cercato di chiedere spiegazioni
a chi poteva saperne di più. E le domande,
come al solito, si facevano insistenti. Poi ho visto
un certo imbarazzo, un certo disagio. « Se non ti va »
ho detto « scusami,
non se ne parli più. » « Ma non è per questo »
mi ha fatto lei. « È che così, a bruciapelo . . .
Preparami, voglio dire,
lasciami tempo di abituarmi. »

— Ma non ci sarà, lo sai bene,
conclusione migliore alla vicenda,
soluzione diversa dal previsto. Solo tutt'al più
primo o poi un tizio che verrà, uno dei soliti,
a portare certi suoi risultati di qualcosa: per esempio pezzi di carte,
foto, testimonianze . . .

5

IL CORPO (il primo, s'intende).
.   .   .   .
Ma poi era venuto su dalle scale
nel buio.
Avrà fatto di certo i cinque piani a piedi.
.   .   .   .
Nascosto nel portaombrelli. Identificato.
Finalmente. Recuperato nel sonno.

4

I'd sought to ask for explanations from
whoever might know more about it. And the questions,
as usual, grew insistent. Then I saw a certain
embarrassment, a certain discomfort. "If you're unhappy with it,"
I said, "excuse me,
I won't talk about it anymore." "But that's not it,"
she told me. "It's just that this way, out of nowhere . . .
Prepare me, I mean to say,
give me time to get used to it."

—But there won't be, as you well know,
a better ending to the incident,
a different solution than what we expect. Only at most
sooner or later some guy who'll come, one of the usual ones,
to bring certain of his results of something: for instance pieces of
         paper,
photos, depositions.

5   .

THE BODY (the first one, I mean).
·   ·   ·   ·   ·   ·   ·   ·   ·   ·   ·   ·

But then he had come up the stairs
in the dark.
He'd surely taken the five floors on foot.
·   ·   ·   ·   ·   ·   ·   ·   ·   ·   ·   ·

Hidden in the umbrella stand. Identified.
At last. Recovered in sleep.

6

Un fischio ha fatto tutto il corridoio (lungo,
credo, una quindicina di metri) crescendo fino in fondo,
sulla porta. Lì, poi, c'è stato qualcos'altro.
Non so.
            Un rumore forte
                        (un vetro rotto?
                                    un vaso caduto?)

6

A whistling noise went the whole length of the hall (a long one,
about fifteen meters, I think) growing louder all the way to the end,
at the door. At that point, then, there was something else.
I don't know.
                A loud noise
                        (a broken window?
                                a fallen vase?)

Il magone

Se mi guardi bene sto già pensando
al giorno non lontano in cui dovrò sgomberare la mia roba di qui
per portare tutto nell'altra casa.
I libri e il pianoforte che ancora non ho imparato a suonare.

E già premedito l'inevitabile magone di cui
potrò dirmi che è la mia parte migliore.

E il pacco, che scarti mentre dici
« qui c'è il pigiama nuovo che ti ho preso per la dote » . . .
Di dietro agli occhi tanto per cambiare
sento la lacrima che sale, ma questa volta
ce la faccio e mi trattengo. Non è questione
d'essere mammone, è che lo spettro
della solitudine ormai doppia (non mia) . . . e quella musica
alla radio della domenica nel primo pomeriggio confessa
e stabilisce la quantità della pena. E qui

di fare il bravo il duro di giocare d'ironia
per non sentirsi dentro
straziare dalla commozione questione . . .
. . . questione non è più ti dico.

The Lump in the Throat

If you look at me closely I'm already thinking
about that day not long from now when I'll have to clear out my
     stuff from here
and cart it all off to the other house.
The books and the piano I still haven't learned how to play.

And I'm already premeditating the inevitable lump in the throat
that I can tell myself is my best part.

And the package, which you toss aside while saying
"here are the new pajamas I bought you as a gift" . . .
From behind my eyes for a change
I feel the tear start rising, but this time
I hang on and hold it back. It's not a matter
of being a mama's boy, it's that the specter
of loneliness is doubling by now (not mine) . . . and that music
on the radio early Sunday afternoon makes a confession
and sets the amount of the punishment. And here

showing off playing the tough guy being ironic
so as not to feel
my insides torn apart over this matter . . .
. . . it doesn't matter anymore I tell you.

Prima parentesi

In fondo ci si può denudare
anche in presenza di terzi. In fondo
si potrebbe far l'amore a tu per tu col nemico . . .
  .   .   .   .
  .   .   .   .

Seconda parentesi

  .   .   .   .
  .   .   .   .
è meglio il tipo che topicca dappertutto,
meglio il mio nonno un po' fattore rovinato dalla guerra e un po'
    tranviere,
che un qualche pirla disinvolto alla James Bond.

First Parenthesis

Basically you can strip naked even
in the presence of third parties. Basically
you could make love face to face with your enemy . . .

. . . .
. . . .

Second Parenthesis

. . . .
. . . .

better the guy who stumbles at every turn,
better my grandfather a little steward ruined by the war and a little
    streetcar driver,
than some uninhibited dickhead á la James Bond.

Figure femminili

1

Le mani in mano.
Concentrazione . . . alla finestra . . .
una sedia. Fuori lo spiazzo . . . i tetti . . .
per l'orto . . . d'estate la siesta.

Dei mobili solo l'impronta sudicia sui muri.
Ma chi gira in vestaglia, al buio,
in anticamera?
Lei? (quale, poi . . .)
Fino alla consumazione dell'atto
portato il gioco, l'incesto.
Rannicchiati al buio in camera
matrimoniale; uno spiraglio, sempre, per la paura
di riaprire gli occhi cieco.

2

Orecchio-occhio, lanterna
magica, sequenza, ancora
per diapositive a ruota libera, forse
sulla sedia a dondolo. Qualche ora.
La cerimonia religiosa (il ritardato arrivo
della testimone, i pochi amici, le firme, le foto
sul sagrato).

Female Figures

1

Thumb-twiddling.
Concentration . . . on the window . . .
a chair. The clearing outside . . . the roofs . . .
through the garden . . . the summer siesta.

Of the furniture only the dirty imprint on the walls.
But who's wandering in a robe, in the dark,
in the entrance hall?
She? (which one, then . . .)
Until the consummation of the act
the game carried on, the incest.
Huddled together in the master
bedroom; always a small crack, out of fear
of blindly reopening our eyes.

2

Ear-eye, magic
lantern, sequence, through
slides in a free-spinning wheel once more,
maybe in a rocking-chair. A few hours.
The religious ceremony (the delayed arrival
of the witness, the few friends, the signatures, the photos
in the churchyard).

Impressioni sovrapposte. In cucina,
rumore di piatti. Tu? Lei? (L'una? L'altra?) Una fase
intermedia?
       (spiegazione della megera che inseguiva, inseguiva,
       questa notte.)
Ma chi avrà assistito al trasporto, alla spoliazione?
La recisione drastica (del resto,
altrimenti, come?) del cordoncino, cruenta
       (fino alla consumazione dell'atto . . .

       . . . .)

3

Di sera . . . la tv . . . sul divano,
raggomitolata: « El mè ninin . . .
El va! »

— Non ho mai pianto tanto. Recidi!
— Hai ragione, aspetta:
A cena, interno di cucina. Il campanello. « Apro. »
. . . ma la sorpresa . . . (stringedone la mano
grossa sulla porta) . . . « vieni » alla madre « . . .
vieni . . . dall'aldilà . . . in carne e ossa . . . lui . . .

È TORNATO."

4

Sulla tavola il pane, i pesci.
I piatti di alluminio.

Overlapping impressions. In the kitchen,
a clamor of plates. You? She? (The one? The other?) An
intermediate stage?

> (explanation of the hag who followed in pursuit
> tonight.)

But who will have witnessed the transport, the pillaging?
The drastic excision (besides,
otherwise, how?) of the cord, all bloody?

> (until the consummation of the act . . .
>
> . . . .)

3

In the evening . . . the TV . . . on the couch,
curled in a ball: "My little boy . . .
There he goes!"

—I've never cried so much. Stop it!
—You're right, wait:
At dinner, in the kitchen. The doorbell. "I'll get it."
. . . but the surprise . . . (shaking his big
hand at the door) . . . "come here" to the mother ". . .
come here . . . from the next world . . . in flesh and blood . . . he . . .

HAS COME BACK."

4

On the table the bread, the fish.
The aluminum plates.

Corte dei miracoli

Non è credibile a sentirlo con le proprie orecchie.
Viverlo — ti capisco — un inferno, una vergogna,

un'ansia di scappare (ma restiamo
nei dettagli più essenziali e meno compiaciuti:

la pianta della sacrestia, le malefatte
arcinote del prevosto, l'untuosità dei coadiutori —

il gobbo e il sordo — e delle suore. Il furto
alle cassette, la pistola,

avvolta nel giornale, il colpo in canna . . .)

Court of Miracles

It's not credible hearing it with your own ears.
Living it—I understand you—a horror, a shame,

an anxiety to escape (but let's stay with
the more essential and less savory details:

the plan of the sacristy, the pastor's well-known
offenses, the unctuousness of his assistants—

the hunchback and the deaf one—and of the nuns.
The stealing from the poor boxes, the pistol,

wrapped in newspaper, the bullet in the barrel . . .)

Monte Sinai

Non dico di no, un pochino, magari,
ci avevo anche pensato (ma, in fondo,
ero talmente poco sveglio . . .). Ma, poi, alla vista lassù in cima
di quel prete nero, mani sui fianchi, sguardo fiero (« cosa fate
voi due alla vostra età,
lì seduti nel prato. E poi è proprietà privata »).
C'era davvero da sprofondarsi? O piuttosto
da ridere e incavolarsi? Resta il fatto che borbottando
ci siamo messi in tasca io e lei nostri fazzoletti
e siamo scesi giù. E ancora non sapendo dove andare (« ma
    guarda tu,
che razza di imbecille. Si stava lì tranquilli. Chi faceva
niente di male? . . . »).

Mount Sinai

I don't say no, a little bit, maybe,
I'd even thought about it (but, basically,
I was hardly awake . . .) But, then, with the sight up there at the
    summit
of that fierce-faced priest in black, hands on his hips ("What are
you two doing sitting there
in the grass at your age? Besides, this is private property").
Was it something we should have been crushed by? Or should we
have laughed and been pissed off? The fact remains that muttering
she and I stuffed our handkerchiefs in our pockets
and headed down the hill. And still not knowing where to go
    ("but look,
what a total imbecile. We were sitting there quietly. Who was doing
anything wrong? . . .")

Libretto personale

1

Visto da fuori più somigliante a un carcere.
Per lo meno accantonati
sgradevoli pensieri di compiti, interrogazioni,
sbirciate sul registro.
(Macchie d'inchiostro sul quaderno. Una puntura,
quasi, uno stringersi — una fitta? L'emozione? —
giù; in basso.)

Nuove didascalie, leggende
per un immaginario album personale;
lo scorrere del film, lo sfogliarsi delle pagine . . .

: « adesso vai avanti lungo il porticato. Poi dal cortile
scorgi l'altoparlante, i finestroni, la porticina
d'ingresso alla cappella.
                              Mettiti in fila
per due, ai primi posti. L'atrio; su
per l'ampia scalinata buia, lenta,
interminabile. »

Personal Booklet

1

Seen from outside looking more like a prison.
Set aside at least
are unpleasant thoughts of duties, interrogations,
peeks at the register.
(*Ink stains on the notebook. A puncture wound,
almost, a tightening—a sharp pain? Emotion?—
low; down.*)

New subtitles, captions
for an imaginary personal album;
the movie running, the pages being turned . . .

: "now move along the portico. Then from the courtyard
you make out the loudspeaker, the great big windows, the little door
that leads into the chapel.
                              Lined up in rows
of two, in the first spots. The entryway; up
along the wide, dark, plodding, endless
flight of stairs."

2

Il magazzino, le matassine colorate. Schede
scarabocchiate. Quotidiana,
mattutina esplorazione tra le lavoranti.

. . . .

. . . .

. . . . E vedo
che cominciava a prender corpo nel silenzio
quel languore dei tre giorni (sui banchi di legno
altissimi riviste, libriccini,
pubblicazioni religiose. Assiduo
il sorvegliare petulante — il naso sulle pagine sottili
sottili del breviario — delle vesti nere).

. . . .

. . . .

Venivo via fingendo febbre, raffreddore,
brividi, abbandonando in preda al panico di cifre
nere, rosse, improbabili, alla mitraglia
della calcolatrice, alle bestemmie (sue), agli assalti
(del principale) il vecchio ragioniere . . .

. . . .

. . . .

Fame, già quasi, lo sgranocchiare del rosario in gruppo,
la via crucis del tramonto, cantilenata, i compagni
distratti, sparpagliati. Poi correre, giocare.

(Salto i gradini due per volta, messo in fuga,
fatto correre dal suocero a ombrellate
su e giù per i tornanti, illuminati a giorno,
solitamente tetri, ora deserti, dei soliti scaloni.)

2

The storeroom, the little colored skeins. Cards
that were scribbled on. Each day
the morning exploration among the workers.

. . . .

. . . .

. . . . And I see
that it began to take shape in the silence,
that three-day listlessness (on the tall
wooden pews magazines, pamphlets,
religious publications. Assiduous
the nagging supervision—nose in the tissue-thin
breviary pages—of the black robes).

. . . .

. . . .

I came away pretending to have a fever,
a cold, chills, abandoning the old accountant
to the panic of black, red, improbable figures,
to the machine-gun of the calculator,
to curses (his), to onslaughts (from the boss) . . .

. . . .

. . . .

Hunger, just about, the crunching of the rosary in a group,
the Via Crucis at sunset, chanted, the classmates
distracted and spread out. Then running and playing.

(I climb the steps two at a time, put to flight,
set to running by the blows of my father-in-law's umbrella
up and down through the hairpin turns, lit up by day,
usually dark, now deserted, of the usual staircases.)

(Ancora i denti — protagonisti? — sbriciolati,
come polvere nel mangiare. O con tenaglie
a strapparmi il piombo dell'otturazione.)

3

È come riassumere, rivedere . . . Così,
bene o male, duplicato, anche mi mangio . . .
Dopo la fuga, a vuoto, effimere consolazioni
le tenerezze riservate al gatto, in poltrona,
l'aiuto di pornogiornali, la tv . . .

Tocco fatale alla benedizione. Incenso
profumato, fumo,
cantare (*o sacrum*
convivium), buio, vibrazioni
d'organo dietro l'altare (*tantum*
ergo) a gran voce
nei banchi sulle ginocchia peste, l'ansia,
ormai spossato, uscendo (*o salutaris*
hostia) quel vuoto, da svenire, in processione,
proprio al stomaco.

4

All'ultimo colpo di fischietto,
fuori dalla cappella sul porticato opposto
le ceste coi famigli:
                    di qui col pane, le brioches; di là
col cioccolato, le marmellatine.

(Again the teeth—protagonists?—still crumbling,
like powder when I'm eating. Or else pulling
the lead of my fillings out with a pair of pliers.)

3

It's how to sum up, to review . . . So that,
for better or worse, a copy, I eat myself up again . . .
After escaping, in vain, the ephemeral comforts
affections reserved for the cat, in the armchair,
the aid of porn magazines, the television . . .

Fatal touch at the benediction. Scented
incense, smoke,
chanting (*o sacrum*
convivium), darkness, vibrations
of the organ behind the altar (*tantum*
ergo) in a loud voice
in the pews on ground-down knees, the anxiety,
exhausted by now, going out (*o salutaris*
hostia) that emptiness, feeling faint, in procession,
in the pit of the stomach.

4

At the last blast of the whistle
outside the chapel on the facing portico
the baskets with the ushers:
                    over here with bread, croissants; over there
with chocolate, jams.

Il principio

Qui non è più il cervello
che detta legge.

Mi sono organizzato ormai
diversamente.

« La testa » dici « mi duole. »
« La *mia* testa » ripeti smorfiando.

. . . : e già ti vedo in pezzi senza scampo
                                    gli attrezzi qua e là.
« Il corpo » dici « il *mio* corpo. »

. . . : e già ti vedo suddiviso analizzato
e già ti scopro dissociante.

In sosta, però, medito:
mi potrei buttare incontrollato.

Esito ancora un po', dubbioso; eccomi
dunque. Ecco, tra panico e frenesia,
vedo!
Come una forma tonda e come un coso sopra.
La lingua? Taccio.
Vedo *due* forme tonde.
È inutile! Non resisto . . .

Sono là sopra . . .

The Principle

Ô mon bien souverain, cher corps, je n'ai que toi!
P. Valéry

Here it's no longer the brain
that lays down the law.

By now I've organized myself
another way.

"My head" you say "is aching."
"*My* head" you repeat grimacing.

. . . : and already I see you inescapably in pieces
                              the implements here and there.
"My body" you say "*my* body."

. . . : and already I see you subdivided analyzed
and already I find you to be dissociating.

Pausing, however, I ponder:
I could plunge right in unchecked.

I still waver a little, doubtful; here I am
then. Here, between panic and frenzy,
I see!
As a round form and a whatchamacallit on top.
The tongue? I keep still.
I see *two* round forms.
It's useless. I don't fight it . . .

I'm up there . . .

Fresia

Come sono cresciute
le bambine . . .
                    L'ho rivisto
nel buio, gli occhi
perfettamente tondi e i grandi baffi ma
soprattutto un avido, pauroso,
vasto sorriso . . . I calzoncini gli cadevano
sotto il ginocchio, le bianche maniche
arrotolate al gomito. E allora,
piccola Gabriella, perché scappare?

Era un pozzo, ero sull'orlo,
proprio sull'orlo del pozzo? « Morto »,
diceva, senza adeguata fama nazionale (pensavo
agli occhi rossi per il vino) eppure
gran giocoliere, padrone chiaro dell'attrezzo
elementare, mancino estroso, precocemente
inghiottito; buffo amico mago
dei bambini o non lui stesso lupo, orco,
avida talpa?

Fresia

How the little girls
have grown . . .
                    I saw him again
in the dark, perfectly
round eyes and huge whiskers but
above all else a greedy, fearful,
broad smile . . . His shorts came down
below the knee, white sleeves
rolled up to the elbow. Well then,
little Gabriella, why run away?

Was he a well, was I on the edge,
on the very edge of the well? "Dead,"
he said, without a suitable national reputation (I thought
of his wine-reddened eyes) and yet
a great juggler, a clear master of a basic
instrument, a whimsical lefty prematurely
swallowed up; a friendly comical wizard
to the children, or not himself a wolf, an ogre,
a greedy mole?

Concorrenze

1

Certo del fatto suo, io lo seguivo, prudente
a debita distanza . . .

L'edificio scolastico, nella campagna (la strada
al sole, senza marciapiede)   (all'interno

idea di animali, che so . . . topi . . .
farfalle . . .)

2

Senza il conforto del paesaggio; né, alla rincorsa,
didascalia, commento musicale; scenario, ambito

vuoto, volgare, indifferente . . . (il prevalere
dell'accidia? Pesce straniero, sbigottito

tra polvere e moschini. Dove la sede,
la fonte all'energia?)

Competitions

1

Sure of his actions, I followed him, discreetly
at a proper distance . . .

The school building, out in the country (the road
in the sun, with no sidewalks)   (inside

a notion of animals, say . . . mice . . .
butterflies . . .)

2

Without the comfort of the landscape; nor, in
the run-up, subtitles, musical commentary; setting,

an empty area, vulgar, indifferent . . . (the triumph
of indolence? A fish out of water, dumfounded

amid the dust and gnats. Where is the seat,
the source of energy?)

3

(Che passeggiava, detective o ladro gentiluomo,
non era necessariamente personaggio noto,

riconoscibile: io, forse tu, diciamo,
fermato dalla cinepresa.)

4

Corridoio o ambulacro; scarti bruschi, sviluppi
di fuga all'azione, inseguimenti premonitori (sguscia

dall'aula la maestra P. giù per i chiostri verdi
— gironi? strapiombi? In caccia

il traduttore C. del pari trafelato.) Osservando, io
spiando ora dalla finestra, in alto,

in disparte, quasi passivo o forse
seguendo un mio disegno . . .

5

Bambini c'indicavano il luogo del congresso . . .

Nella maratona per i campi col collega
camuso, appiccicoso il clima, appesantito

nella digestione, nell'estremo
sforzo podistico.

3

(The one walking by, detective or gentleman thief,
was not necessarily a known, recognizable

character; me, or maybe you, let's say,
caught by the movie camera.)

4

Hallway or ambulatory; sudden swerves, developments
from flight to action, premonitory chases (the schoolmistress

P. slips away from the classroom down through green cloisters
—rings? precipices? In pursuit

the translator C. equally out of breath.) I, watching,
spying now from the window, up high,

apart, more or less passive or perhaps
following one of my plans . . .

5

Children showed us where the conference was . . .

In the marathon through the fields with a snub-nosed
colleague, the weather clammy, weighed down

with digestion, in the extreme
effort of walking.

6

L'edificio scolastico (ma gli animali?)

I volti: l'attore consumato, la virago,
la suffragetta (spregiudicati), Buffalo Bill; seri,

dignitosi, autentici: bidelli,
inservienti, portinai (composti). Il dialettico

dai denti cavallini (contraffatta, residua
o dominante tensione agonistica; alle labbra

come vomito giallo, dalla bocca
sdentata, tale

da insudiciare la traversa, scuotere
l'ago infilzato nella vena . . .)

7

La mia « mozione »? . . . Esplicita l'insidia, l'agguato,
l'invito al cimento (« misurati, cogli l'applauso »).

« Se non senti . . . cosa vuoi dire . . .
È come definire senza capire . . . »
                    Secco, provocatorio: « La questione
non verte qui circa il sesso degli angeli ».
« Peccato. »

6

The school building (but the animals?)

The faces: the consummate actor, the virago,
the suffragette (all open-minded), Buffalo Bill; serious,

dignified, authentic: janitors,
custodians, porters (composed). The dialectician

with the horse teeth (a counterfeit, residual
or prevailing competitive tension; at the lips

like yellow vomit, from the toothless
mouth, so as

to stain the drawsheet, to jiggle
the needle jammed in the vein . . .)

7

My "motion"? . . . The snare obvious, the ambush,
the call to the challenge ("test yourself, reap the applause").

"If you're not hearing . . . what you're meaning . . .
It's like explaining without understanding . . ."
                        Dry, provocative: "The question
here doesn't bear upon the sex of angels."
"Too bad."

8

Le mani sudate, i polpastrelli
sbocconcellati e neri. « Eccomi, eccomi

di ritorno, io stesso muto spettro,
sia pure, istrione, commediante
discreto, antagonista subdolo, sia pure . . .
. . . non so la mia classifica, se il mio prestigio

ne sia diminuito, uscito scosso. » Vincitore o vinto,
pochi di loro (alibi

o giustificazione), infine,
in carne e ossa.

8

The hands sweaty, the fingertips
nibbled and black. "Here I am, here I am

come back, myself a silent ghost,
granted, a histrionic, a passable
comedian, a crafty antagonist, granted . . .
. . . I don't know my ranking, if my standing's

diminished by it, shaken up." Conqueror or conquered,
few of them (alibi

or justification), in the end,
in flesh and blood.

da LE MERAVIGLIE DELL'ACQUA (1980)

from THE WONDERS OF WATER (1980)

con una bocca ancora

con una bocca ancora dolce umida
come altre volte certi spalancati occhi, dopo
un'ultima rassicurante stretta uscendo,
capire ripetendo mentalmente o a fior di labbra
per le scale, lentamente, imbambolato
per la strada . . . : questo e altri disagi . . .
scambi di idee a lieto fine . . . sempre, qualche
insulto molta comprensione e scoprire che sei,
sorellina, un'altra persona da me.

with a mouth sweet once more moist
like certain other times eyes wide open, leaving
after one last reassuring embrace,
understanding repeating mentally or in a whisper
along the stairs, slowly, drowsily
along the road . . . : this and other discomforts . . .
swaps of ideas with a happy ending . . . always, a few
insults a lot of comprehension and discovering that you,
little sister, are a different person from me.

Letargo

1

Il gran piacere dell'accidia . . . scivola, si appallottola
nella boccia di vetro; magari contemplando
le meraviglie del vetrino, lo svolgersi della vita nel letargo,
nella vacanza . . .

quasi di colpo mi sto portando a pari degli altri.

2

Quel solito gelato ripugnante,
denso; quella crema dolciastra . . .

ricordo lo sfarzo della sotterranea:
« ma non fidarti — mi diceva uno —
presto si ferma, ti lascia a metà strada . . . »

Hibernation

1

The great pleasure of sloth . . . he glides, he curls up in a ball
in the glass bowl; maybe contemplating the wonders
under the microscope, how life goes on in hibernation,
on vacation . . .

almost at once I'm acting just like the others.

2

That usual thick disgusting
gelato; that sickly-sweet custard . . .

I recollect the splendor of the subway:
"Don't count on it," somebody said to me,
"It stops suddenly, it leaves you halfway there . . ."

3

Mi eri forse nemica per turbati segni . . .

al diavolo le moine del gatto (ti aggredisco,
fazioso, certo vilmente) . . . a tavola
strizzavi l'occhio a un tizio
e via di questo passo . . .

ti scrivo.

4

Mostriciattolo d'autista . . . arrogante, odioso;
quei pochi peli d'una barbetta rossiccia . . . passeggiavo
su e giù; dopo la sosta, ecco il battello andarsene:
solo per poco in fumo la mia gita solitaria,
nel mistero ancora la destinazione.

5

Domina nascosta, invisibile,
il pietoso, sconosciuto osservatore: ne dedurrà
le fasi essenziali, tipiche:
nel corpo umano quel lungo giacere quasi immobile . . .

l'identità delle visioni,
possibili metafore gratuite . . .
i succhi interni, pappa vischiosa che ristagna,
da assimilare, distribuire, espellere.

3

You might have been hostile toward me through troubled signals . . .

the hell with this pussyfooting (I assail you,
unfairly, really vilely) . . . at the table
you winked your eye at some guy
and so on and so forth . . .

I write to you.

4

A little monster of a driver . . . arrogant and obnoxious;
those scraggly hairs of a reddish-brown goatee . . . I was strolling
up and down; after parking the car, the boat heading out:
for just a little while my solitary trip up in smoke,
the destination still a mystery.

5

Hidden, invisible, he dominates,
the compassionate, unknown observer: he'll infer
the typical basic stages:
in the human body that long, almost motionless idling . . .

the sameness of the sights,
possible gratuitous metaphors . . .
internal juices, sticky pap that clots,
to be absorbed, distributed, expelled.

6

Fare del moto, questo il consiglio . . .

parlo per voce di un estraneo, un amico . . .
facce che tendono a scomporsi, fondersi; gli intrusi
si moltiplicano . . . i ruffiani, ambigue
fisionomie multiple . . .

belluino, scimmiesco, folto di sopracciglia
d'improvviso sulla fronte, l'innocuo, piccolo C.,
cresciuto a dismisura, lo sguardo, il sorriso,
già ebete, pauroso . . .

7

Oltre quei monti
sono altri monti — disse — e altri ancora:
nudi, tremendi, inabitati; d'intatti abeti . . .
e lo scrosciare dei torrenti . . . di valle in valle:
null'altro che i miei passi, i sandali.

8

Riesco a tenere ferma la scrittura,
controllata nella mano sulla lettera,
fieramente . . .

oscillo incerto
tra dentro e fuori: l'eroe . . . la formica . . .
l'antica profondità epistolare . . .

6

The recommendation: take some exercise . . .

I speak with the voice of an outsider, a friend . . .
faces that tend to decompose, to melt; the intruders
multiply . . . the pimps, shifty
multiple physiognomies . . .

savage, apelike, dense eyebrows suddenly
there on his forehead, harmless little C.,
grown enormously, the look, the smile,
now scary and moronic . . .

7

Beyond these mountains
are other mountains—he said—and others still:
bare, fearsome, uninhabited; with untouched firs . . .
and the roaring of the torrents . . . from valley to valley:
nothing else around but my steps, my sandals.

8

I manage to maintain a steady hand
over the letter, keeping the writing firm,
proudly . . .

I swing uncertainly
between inside and out: the hero . . . the ant . . .
old-time epistolary profundity . . .

9

Pochi barlumi: un tailleur chiaro a righe, un certo
sapore voluttuoso nella bocca, socchiusa, ammorbidita,
gonfia . . .

non basta la parola fine nel risveglio;
soddisfazione occorre già dal sonno;
appagamento pieno . . .

difficile decidersi, muoversi e andare,
tra latte e sporcizia, nel verde dei Grasselli . . .

10

Prendeva a correre, a correre . . . veniva su tra i prati, la cascina,
crescendo d'evidenza, dimensioni . . . con maggiore affanno:
        mosso,
convulso in primo piano, quasi in rilievo, tanto
da soffocarmi, annaspando, cadermi addosso . . .

bene o male, poi, si sarebbe ridestato.

(sulla cima
è ancora zona indefinibile, terra di nessuno . . . più in là
— ma i lottatori, dalla notte,
avrebbero ripreso nuove forze —
è come rotolare verso il mare,
immergersi . . .)

9

A few glimmers: a bright striped pantsuit, a certain
sensuous taste swells in the half-open, softened
mouth . . .

the delicate word at waking's not enough;
now satisfaction has to come from sleep;
total fulfillment . . .

hard to make up your mind, to get up and go,
amid the milk and dirt, in the Grasselli park . . .

10

He began running, running . . . he came up amid the fields, the
        farmhouse,
growing in presence, dimensions . . . out of breath: he moved,
convulsive up close, almost in relief, to practically
throttle me, flailing, falling on top of me . . .

then he would more or less revive.

(on the summit
it's still an unmarked territory, a no man's land . . . further on
—but by night the fighters
would have regained new might—
it's like rolling toward the sea
and plunging in . . .)

partiamo dall'imparziale rifugio
dai colorati cartoncini da vergare
mentre la morbida mela scivolava
docilmente dal suo imbuto, ripercorrendo
mentalmente l'interminabile scalinata
dei cappuccini . . . accogli degnamente questi
memorabili segnali poiché tu sai
che misteriosi non sono.

we depart from the impartial shelter
made of colored pieces of ruled cardboard
while the pulpy apple slipped
softly from its funnel, mentally
retracing the neverending flight of stairs
of the Capuchins . . . accept them properly,
these memorable signals, since you know
they're not mysterious.

Personaggi

Proiettato sull'esterno, la serie delle case . . .

la piatta, verde sequenza dei prati . . . eccoci
a un'inconsueta forma di presente . . .
(saranno teneri, saranno giusti
questi bacetti adolescenti, saranno
leggerezza opportuna, lecita?)
Con occhi e cuore aperto
riconsidero le cose. Ovattato
da una precoce senilità,
che ricomponga i conflitti, che plachi
le inimicizie e i rancori. Come uno scarto
imprevedibile, un trasgredire distratto,
amico, nell'intimo, banale copiarsi
identico delle stagioni . . .

Attimi di benessere senza tempo, pochi . . .
Gioco un po' sibillino, notturno,
il tardivo svelarsi, tradirsi,
oltre lo schermo, delle due vecchie
sgangherate galline tornite.
Vede il suo naso mentre legge, sfodera
una gaiezza inedita, eccessiva.

Il ticchettio dell'orologio appena aperti gli occhi . . . uno spiraglio
     dalla gelosia . . . lo stridere, passeggero, del piccione sul vetro.
     Anni fa, sulla panchina, nel chiostro già quasi in vacanza; o al
     Museo della Scienza, la riunione dei piloti . . .

Cast of Characters

Projected on the outside, the series of houses . . .

the flat, green sequence of meadows . . . here we are
all at once in an unaccustomed form . . .
(will they be tender, will they be proper,
these little teenage kisses, will they be
a licit, opportune felicity?)
With open heart and eyes
I reconsider things. Muffled by
a premature senility,
that reconciles old clashes, that assuages
enmities and resentments. Like an unforeseeable
discarding, an absentminded amicable
transgression, in an intimate banal imitation
just like the seasons . . .

Moments of timeless well-being, few of them . . .
A nighttime game, a bit mysterious,
the belated offscreen
revealing, betraying of two old
ramshackle turned hens.
He sees his nose while reading, he displays
a new and quite excessive merriment.

The ticking of the clock as soon as you open your eyes . . . a glimmer
from the blinds . . . the fleeting screech of a pigeon on the glass.
Years ago, on a bench, in the cloister already practically on
vacation; or at the Museum of Science, the pilots' reunion . . .

L'orrore degli sputi freschi,
nel gelo dei pochissimi passanti . . .
La Villa Reale, il grande parco . . .
Un'altra stagione i cavalli,
i lazzaroni che giocano a golf.
Vedevo bei quadretti, lingotti
di zucchero candido.
                    Mutano
gli oggetti, finalmente, si fanno
elettrici, più luminosi.
Nei camion che sfilavano,
montagne di foglie secche . . .
                    del paesino, visto dall'alto
m'incantava la semplice regolarità delle strade,
le basse case con l'orto, l'assoluta
tranquillità, assenza di traffici.

Ma lo slancio tendeva a trasformarsi in smarrimento . . . o nel solito
        disagio inconcludente (: « Consolati, di te, che sei stonata, non
        si dirà, *quella che canta sempre* »): così da solo, lamentandosi,
        quasi
piagnucolando (: « Accidenti . . . come si vive male . . . »)

Che non funzioni più l'archivio?
Lo so,
l'abitudine non è un conforto.

Così noi due, personaggi scipiti,
circolavamo un po' nell'ombra, un po' nella memoria.

The horror of fresh spittle,
in the frost of the few passersby . . .
Villa Reale, the grand park . . .
In another season the horses,
the layabouts playing golf.
I saw delightful little squares, nuggets
of white sugar.
                    In the end
the objects change, they become
electric, more luminous.
In the trucks that went past,
mountains of dry leaves . . .
                              seen from up above, the simple
regularity of the village streets, the low houses with
kitchen gardens, the absolute tranquility
and the lack of traffic all enchanted me.

But the impulse had a way of turning into confusion . . . or into the
    usual inconclusive uneasiness (: "Console yourself, you who
    are out of tune, that they won't call you *that woman who's
    always singing*"): so alone, moaning, almost
sniveling (: "Damn . . . how wretchedly we live . . .")

The archive isn't open anymore?
I know,
habit isn't any comfort now.

And so we two, insipid characters,
moved along somewhat in shadow, somewhat in memory.

Il buio, le luci e l'arcobaleno

1

. . . quella mia stessa immagine, perciò,
scoperta nelle luci, nei rumori
elettrici all'Arena.

(quali giri misteriosi, insomma? labirintici
passaggi, spargendo
meravigliosi messaggi, oscuri cenni da . . .

tu sparivi, dopo la come sempre minuziosa,
lenta esposizione di un pensiero, di un
ricordo . . . mi attiravano molto
le figurine di cartone)

Girando la chiavetta, la rana
balla tutto intorno . . .

Cerchi di buio caldi,
ispessendosi; la mia schiena
dolcemente intiepidita e umida; nell'azione,
l'ombreggiatura degli spigoli,
le punte acuminate dello sguardo
proteso, verso il fondo dell'imbuto:

le evoluzioni
sarebbero arrivate fino al grido.

The Dark, the Lights and the Rainbow

1

. . . that image of me, therefore, the same one
uncovered in the lights, in the electric
noises of the Arena.

(those mysterious turns, then? labyrinthine
passages, scattering
marvelous messages, dark traces from . . .

you disappeared, after the as always meticulous,
slow exposition of a thought, of a
memory . . . I was very drawn to those
pasteboard picture cards)

With the turning of the little key, the frog
dances all around . . .

Hot, thickening
circles of darkness; my back
softly warmed and damp; in action,
the shading of the corners,
the sharp tips of my gaze
outstretched, toward the bottom of the funnel:

developments
would have gone as far as an outcry in the end.

2

Non c'è abbastanza aria . . . apri . . .
non c'è luce . . . gli astanti più vicini,
maschere . . . Mi soffoca, mi opprime.
Al centro il ruolo dei modelli,
si esprime il padrone delle luci, il grande
airone impennato; sormonto dalle ruote, dal
telaio, nella lucentezza invitante del celeste,
discreta, il buio cupo dei gradini. O nondimeno

il gioco pallido del volto, il roteare
assurdo dei suoi occhi, le labbra fini, gli scatti
secchi, ritmici del collo, i lapsus,
i proverbi, quel nomignolo . . . Comparse

alla ribalta, dunque, come si legge.
Passeggeri inattesi, pronti al pubblico,
essi stessi spettatori; i grossi occhi
umidi, rotondi, in gentilissimo agguato,
le grassocce mani tozze: Celestino,
dal pianerottolo . . . sì, i dolciumi, sudato,
sorridente. Anche
il falegname donnaiolo, amico
delicato, il
cappellaio . . .

2

There's not enough air . . . open up . . .
there's no light . . . the nearest bystanders,
masks . . . It smothers me, oppresses me.
At the heart of it the role of the models,
the master of the lights, great feathered heron,
expresses himself; I rise from the wheels, the frame,
in the discreet, inviting sky-blue brightness,
the gloomy dark of the stairs. Or notwithstanding

his pale joke of a face, the ridiculous
rolling of his eyes, his thin lips, his neck's
rhythmic, abrupt jerks, his slips of the tongue,
his sayings, and that nickname . . . He emerged

into the limelight then, just as we've read.
Unexpected travelers, ready for the public,
spectators themselves: their great big round
damp eyes, in an extremely tender ambush;
the plump and stumpy hands; Celestino,
from the landing . . . yes, the candies,
sweaty, smiling. Also
the ladykiller carpenter, delicate
friend, the
hatmaker . . .

3

Uno scricchiolio delle tavole, nient'altro . . . Vacillo,
però, assordato (il bianco costume come nelle foto,
nel fotogramma, l'affanno dell'ascesa, il tremito
violento, la voce altissima, alla finestra, i brividi

nel grido). Non tengo, tutto s'inclina, rumoreggia, apre
varchi, fischi immaginari, buio, fuga precipitosa di persone. « Ma
è assurdo! — grido — è assurdo, inspiegabile! » Eppure ridono
le mie facce: beffarde, geometriche; indelebili
occhietti che s'imprimono, puntuti; sono già
malfide, aggressive . . . storpi
paurosi a non finire . . . È un vigliacco,
un vigliacco chi li proietta . . .

                              Un imprevisto scenico? Può essere.
O la chiave tragica della finzione . . .
Tra le diverse maschere (già riassorbiti, ecco,
annullati nell'ombra, dalle quinte,
quei più modesti ruoli: come i modelli, comunque,
gli stessi eroi) . . . proprio la mia,

senza ricorso a . . . Ho chiara
l'immagine . . . come sempre,
meno chiaro il concetto . . . il senso. L'ordine . . .
naturale (?) delle cose
concretamente propone i rapporti;
predispone, aggredisce rifiutato.

3

A creaking of the boards, nothing else . . . I waver,
however, deafened (the white costume as in the photos,
in the frame, the breathlessness of the ascent, the violent
trembling, the very high voice, at the window, the shivers

in the outcry). I'm not holding on, everything tilts, rumbles,
    opens up
passages, imaginary catcalls, darkness, a mad rush of people. "But
it's absurd," I shout, "it's absurd, inexplicable!" And yet my faces
are laughing: mocking, geometrical; indelible eyes
that imprint themselves, sharply; already they're
treacherous, aggressive . . . scary
unending cripples . . . It's a coward,
a coward who projects them . . .

                                An unexpected scene? It just might be.
Or else the tragic key of makebelieve . . .
Among the different masks (already reabsorbed, here,
cancelled in the shadow, from the wings,
those smaller roles: like the models, in any case,
the heroes themselves) . . . really my own,

without recourse to . . . I have the image
clear . . . as always,
less clear the concept . . . the sense. The natural (?)
order . . . of things
pragmatically proposes all the terms;
arranges; rejected, it attacks.

4

Si viaggiava attorno . . . ma non
con moto
uniforme; a balzi, piuttosto,
a scosse
vertiginose . . . ogni giro, ormai,
sembrava avvicinarci lentamente
al fondo; però in modo sensibilissimo.

Ero già al calcolo delle forme,
delle geometriche parvenze che sprofondano;

gorgogliavo senza sosta, senza
respiro dentro; tra i rottami, laggiù,
qualcosa dev'esserci stato, non capivo . . .
qualcosa . . . non c'è dubbio . . . Ma come proteggersi,
nell'annaspare ridicolo, aggrapparsi
a un troppo lontano, rassicurante corpo . . .

5

Poi, le rotazioni divennero
a grado a grado meno veloci. La schiuma
e l'arcobaleno poco alla volta dileguarono
e il fondo di quel baratro apparve lentamente
evolversi. Riportando l'attore
a occhi aperti, gli avanzi della scena.

4

We traveled around . . . but not
with a steady
motion; by leaps, instead,
by dizzying
jolts . . . every turn, by then,
seemed to be slowly drawing us nearer to
the bottom; but in the most sensitive manner.

I was already calculating shapes,
the geometric appearances that collapse;

I babbled on without a pause, without
drawing a breath; down there, amid the wreckage,
something had to have been there, I didn't understand . . .
something . . . there's no doubt . . . But so as to protect itself,
in the ridiculous floundering, clutching at
a far too distant, reassuring body . . .

5

Then after that, the rotations became
gradually less rapid. All the froth
and the rainbow dispersed a little at a time
and the bottom of that chasm seemed to be slowly
growing. Carrying back the open-eyed
actor, and the residue of the scene.

da GLENN (1982)

from GLENN (1982)

Viaggio di Glenn

Sedevo distratto sul gradino nero
della statua le spalle già rivolte
al lago quando ho capito che era lì
in grande affanno a darmi il suo

saluto . . . Ancora biondi erano
i suoi capelli eppure mi sentivo
come immobile senza poterle offrire
in cambio che il mio sguardo bruno

e già profondo, luminoso . . . Partivamo

e benché la distanza da quei luoghi
fosse estrema il clima la gente ruvida
inospitale avevamo vesti troppo leggere
scarpe e cappelli di pezza come ti ho raccontato:

avremmo rubato nelle case dalle pentole.

***

Con l'ubriacone sull'auto godevo
lo sterminato squallore della Russia.
Sentivo poi il braccio come mi cadesse
nella polvere macchiando la divisa.

Glenn's Journey

I was sitting absentmindedly on the black
step of the statue my shoulders already turned
toward the lake when I realized that she was
standing there all out of breath and waiting

to greet me . . . Her hair was still blonde
but even so I could feel how motionless
I was and couldn't tender anything
in return except my dark look now already

deep and luminous . . . We started away

and even though it was a long long way
from these parts the climate the coarse
inhospitable people we were too lightly dressed
shoes and hats in tatters just as I've told you:

we would have filched from saucepans in the houses.

***

There with the drunk in the car I was enjoying
the endlessness of the dreariness of Russia.
And I could feel his arm then as it fell
on me in the dust staining my uniform.

Spero che arriverò sfinito sfiancato
tra le foglie a mucchi (pensavo) ho già
paura ho un puntino di sangue che si allarga
vicino all'iride. « Sono gli ippocastani . . .

guarda i colori la luce la sapienza
degli architetti . . . che peccato
non esserci più » notava l'amico
del cuore. In tasca maneggiavo

il passaporto un coltellino dal manico
di legno chiaro . . . eppure attorno cresceva
nettamente progrediva
l'economia infallibile della stagione.

***

Oltre l'enorme finestra nel grigio
aperto delle nubi e del fiume osservavo
il ponte i lampioni la facciata
verde del palazzo ma soprattutto in mia attesa

la nave.

Cercavo l'opposta sponda del golfo e l'autista
non era che un punto nero lontano
dentro l'auto nel vento nella piazza . . .

tornando a voce alta pensavo:
come le bestie gli adulti non ridono mai.

***

I hope that I'll arrive worn out done in
amid the heaps of leaves (I was thinking) I'm
afraid and I've got a spot of blood near my iris
that's getting bigger. "Those are horse-chestnut trees . . .

look at the colors the light the wisdom of
the architects . . . what a pity not to be
here anymore" noted my dear friend.
Inside my pocket I ran my fingers over

my passport a little knife with a handle made
of light-colored wood . . . and yet all around me there
was growing and clearly progressing
the infallible economy of the season.

***

Beyond the enormous window in the wide open
gray of the clouds and the river I observed
the bridge the streetlamps and the green façade
of the palace but more than anything else as I waited there

the ship.

I scanned the opposite shore of the gulf and the driver
was nothing more than a faraway black dot
inside the car in the wind in the square . . .

turning at a loud voice I thought:
like the animals the grownups never laugh.

***

Camminare su una pellicola su un vuoto
secco involucro . . . appoggiato al parapetto
sul canale mi vedevo inghiottire le fiamme
passarmi spavaldo la torcia sul petto

girare fra i tavolini con il violino
e una giacca blu da marinaio . . . sicuramente
sarà stato il padre a iniziarlo e non questo
meschino ciccione che fora tessere e coltiva rape.

***

Ci penso adesso ero al tuo fianco
al tuo seguito ma ti guidavo
nella campagna di grano. Non ho più anelli
alle mie mani e siamo soli lontani

a sgusciare succhiare questi bagnati
frutti. Solo uno scatto additava il suo volto
la nera Bentley sul paese il disegno
arido compatto delle mura . . . guardavo lui la lamina

di verde morto e oltre il mercato il fiume
dove non c'era il ponte di Van Gogh. Ricordi
nanina il secchiello meccanico che ci portava?

***

Curvando tre volte dopo il più debole
squillo notturno ecco quegli occhi
fissi la mano salendo i quattro gradini
oltre la porta una specie di cattedra

Walking on a film on an empty dry
shell . . . as I leaned over the parapet
of the canal I saw myself swallowing flames
defiantly passing myself the torch at my breast

going around the little tables with the fiddle
and a blue sailor's jacket . . . it must have been
the father who initiated him and not this
fat wretch who punches tickets and grows turnips.

***

I think about it now I was at your side
in your wake but I was guiding you
through the wheatfield. I no longer have
rings on my fingers and we're alone far away

shucking and sucking the juice of these
wet fruits. Just one snapshot showed his face
the black Bentley out in the country the compact
plain design of the walls . . . I looked at him the patina

of dead green and past the marketplace the river
where Van Gogh's bridge wasn't. Pumpkin do you recall
the small mechanical bucket that carried us?

***

Bending three times after the very faintest
ringing in the night here are those staring
eyes the hand ascending the four steps
beyond the door a sort of teacher's desk

i pochi resti e le piume . . . facevo luce
scarsa dalla candela tra le gabbie oblique
e il tetto mentre strisciava impolverato
il fagotto . . . sono un pover'uomo (mi dico)

spunto sul taccuino tremante
i pochi giorni che mancano al ritorno . . .
non basta più si appanna questo
gusto animale che mi trascina.

***

Altrove . . . regione notturna regione
dello sconforto, più vive
sono le cose senza nome aperte . . .
già grido di lontano, aspettami! stupito

di chi dirà scappando non ti conosco . . .
proteggimi sarò paziente . . . non mancherò:
non ho più labbra.

the few remains and the feathers . . . I conjured up
a bit of light from the candle between the slanting
cages and the roof while my bundle of dust
crawled on . . . I'm a poor devil (I tell myself)

with trembling hand I mark on the calendar
the few days left till I come home again . . .
it's not enough anymore it's growing dim
this animal gusto dragging me along.

***

Elsewhere . . . a region of night a region of
discomfort, those open
nameless things are more alive . . . already
I cry from the distance, wait for me! astonished

by those who'll say *I don't know you* as they flee . . .
protect me I'll be patient . . . I won't fail:
I no longer have lips.

da DONNA DEL GIOCO (1987)

from MISTRESS OF THE GAME (1987)

Donna del gioco

Così sarai tuttor donna del giuoco
(*Il Fiore*, CLVI)

Il padre che mi parlava
era un ragazzo dal largo sorriso
e aveva gli occhi che hanno già imparato
rifugio lui ristoro mio pensante
che riempie la mia sorte.
Non ti ho tradito ma non ti sogno più
e se mi sogno mi sogno col tuo viso:
sul tuo torace mi ergo
nella tua mano mi fido
con te la folla si spalanca.
Sii maledetto tu
che sai fare e non sai fare
sono un bambino ignavo
che non si vuole alzare.

***

Il cuore vuoto è appeso dietro quieto
compagno minaccioso che non bussa.
« Distratto amante e casuali carezze
il tuo accudirmi solo estremo
ma un po' di società di gioco e ridere
le mie guance così pallide adesso
i bei cavèi el spècc . . . e 'sto musin . . .
Ah! come son mutata . . . »

***

Mistress of the Game

The father who'd talk to me
was a boy with broad grin
and he had eyes that had already learned
I shelter in him I refresh my thinking
that fills in my fate.
I haven't betrayed you but I no longer dream of you
and if I dream of myself I dream myself with your face:
I raise myself on your chest
I entrust myself into your hand
with you the crowd opens up.
Damn you
you who know and don't know what to do
I'm a slothful little boy
who doesn't want to get up.

***

The empty heart is quietly hanging back
a threatening companion who doesn't knock.
"An inattentive lover and chance caresses
your taking care of me the only excess
but a bit of company of games and laughter
my cheeks so pale just now the lovely hair
the looking-glass . . . and this pretty little face . . .
Ah! how I've changed . . ."

***

Il mio costume nero
era cucito a mano ma la maschera
non si sa mai cosa nasconde.
Chissà chi sei donna del gioco
che per mano mi tieni
che mi aspiri e governi
passerò tutto intero
passerò con la testa
in ascolto e presente assoluto.
Il guscio è polpa che si scuote e non c'è più
e anch'io mi sciolgo!
pelli morbide che tremano
urlando poca ombra vuoto grappoli
la forza vita delle donne.
Così vorrei ma il mondo
non è un intreccio della fantasia.

***

Dicevi: è una notte calda
proteggiamo l'entrata, i solitari
viaggiano sulle foglie morte
nei sentieri. Picchiava nel vetro
ma placido diceva: au revoir
au revoir monsieur non sono un ladro
ho smarrito la via diluvia
e il mirto cigola che fa paura.
Aspetto l'ansia lucida del giorno
che seleziona la morte.

***

My black costume
was sewn by hand but the mask
one never knows just what it's covering up.
Who knows who you are mistress of the game
who takes me by the hand
who favors and controls me
I'll come through wholly intact
I'll come through with my brain
attentive and absolutely alert.
The shell's a pulp that's shaken and is gone
and even I dissolve!
soft skins that quiver
howling a small shadow a space clusters
the life force of women.
So I would have it but the world
is not a woven plot of fantasy.

**

You said: it's a hot night,
we'd better guard the entryway, there are people
walking all alone over dead leaves
along the paths. He pounded on the glass
but he spoke calmly when he said: *au revoir*
au revoir monsieur I'm not a thief
I seem to have lost my way it's pouring rain
and it's scary how the myrtle tree is creaking.
I await the lucid anxiety of the day
that chooses death.

**

Un guizzo di luce latita
passa la pelle e si rivela
ma il pensiero non ha parole
è suono o vista
un punto luminoso che sa tutto.
Mi salverò
spoglie opache adorato
volto reso al suo arcaico disegno
in una notte invernale
di grugniti e sudore
non sarò più
l'ospite frettoloso.

***

Una madre che va su polare
e poi va via. Ad abbracciarmi.
E invece solo chimica, umano
soggetto di ferma, soccorso
e lascito orrizontale
pena dissolta in un giorno di pace
poca parola di me.

***

Qualcuno ti cammina
sulla pietra del tetto della testa
tendi le braccia e non la cancelli
la tua orbita cava la tua tenebra di terra
radente luce immobile Matera
Botescià cieco solitario nella fenditura.

A flash of light absconds
passes through the skin and reveals itself
but the thought has no words
it's a sound or a sight
a luminous point that comprehends everything.
I'll save myself
dull spoils an adored
face restored to its archaic design
on a winter night
of grunts and sweat
I'll no longer be
the hasty guest.

***

A mother who rises freezing
and then goes away. To embrace me.
And yet only chemistry, human
subject to confirmation, rescue
and a horizontal legacy
sorrow melted away in a day of peace
scant word of me.

***

Someone's walking
on the stone of your roof of your head
you hold your arms out and you don't efface her
your hollow eye-socket your earthy dark
skimming light motionless Matera
Botescià blind and all alone in the crevice.

O mio pallido birichino
l'orso nero di fuoco è nella gola
c'è il giocattolo di legno marino
e pochissima scienza.
Non vedrò più Milano
lavami lavami lavami.

O my whitefaced little rogue
the black bear of fire is in your throat
there's the toy made out of wood from the sea
and very little science.
I won't see Milan again
cleanse me cleanse me cleanse me.

Lettera e preghiera

Ti bagnerò la fronte come un cane
ti asciugherò la fronte con un bacio.

Caro perduto Luigi
sei oggi più tenero, inerme fratello,
nel mio mutato pensiero.
È bianca la tua pelle, come carta,
e io ci scrivo.
È questo il saluto e sarà più leggero
il sacrificio dell'anima.
Sul lieto silenzio di un prato
si posa l'ombra dell'ultima parola.
Abbi comunque pace
e l'abbia chi ha taciuto. Siamo noi
il corpo dell'economia.

***

Ricompogno il suo volto per sempre,
provvidenza maligna che ci assisti.
Oh che strana farfalla nell'iride,
e la benda che porto è la mia disciplina,
il suo tatuaggio su me.

Un dolce mattino di maggio
avrà visto terre lontane, i partigiani.
Chissà a chi avrà pensato,
in ultimo.

***

Letter and Prayer

I'll wash your forehead like a dog
I'll dry your forehead with a kiss.

Dear lost Luigi
you're tenderer today, defenseless brother
in my altered thinking.
Your skin is white, like paper,
and I'm writing there.
This is the greeting and the sacrifice
of the soul will be lighter.
On the happy silence of a meadow
the shadow of the last word settles.
Be at peace nonetheless
and peace to the one who was silent. It is we
who are the body of economy.

***

I reconstruct his face forever,
malignant providence that watches us.
Oh what a strange butterfly in the iris,
and the bandage I'm wearing is my discipline,
his tattoo on me.

One sweet May morning
he'll have seen faraway places, partisans.
Who knows who it is he'll have thought of,
at the end.

***

Ora il suo volto
è diventato la mia maschera.
Ciò che di lui sapevo
io l'ho versato in me.
Vado via anch'io,
figura umana in panni d'epoca
che non si pensa più.

Now his face
has turned into my mask.
What I knew of him
I have poured into myself.
I'm going away as well,
a human figure in the clothes of a time
one no longer thinks about.

Nel mio felice anno

a Valeria, a Enrico

Le point noir que j'étais, dans la pâle immensité
des sables, comment lui vouloir du mal?
Beckett

et que la mort me treuve plantant mes chous
Montaigne

Nel mio felice anno
l'esordio mi puliva il sentimento
e anche il mattino mi faceva gola.
Ma il possibile vasto è infanzia,
odore di sé, rosario per la vigilia.
Scorro via, sono acqua . . .
Avrai per compagna un'anima comune.

***

Ti guardavo seduta in pace
in un'ora di bosco e dolce pendio.
Ti poserò la mano sulla fronte.
Penso alla tua fatica,
penso al percorso, al firmamento, al debito.
Non ti cucire più:
la pietà cresce la devozione.

***

In My Happy Year

to *Valeria*, to *Enrico*

Le point noir que j'étais, dans la pâle immensité
des sables, comment lui vouloir du mal?
Beckett

et que la mort me treuve plantant mes chous
Montaigne

In my happy year
its opening cleansed all my sentiment
and morning was mouth-watering as well.
But the breadth of what is possible is childhood,
a good name, and a rosary for the vigil.
I flow away, I'm water . . .
You'll have a fellow soul for company.

***

I watched you sitting peacefully
in a time of woodland and a gentle slope.
I'll place a hand upon your brow.
I think about your weariness,
I think about the journey, heaven, duty.
Don't sew anymore:
compassion reintensifies devotion.

***

Vedevo dal villaggio il campanile
e la rampa bagnata. Solo un guizzo
per essere lassù, in prima fila.
Ma il cuore della parola
si disfa e mi avvelena.
Meglio il cliente attardato
che si rialza e ride:
« Fiorirà un altro uomo — pensa —
non volerò a picco
nell'afa, nell'ombra morta,
nelle caverne del fondovalle . . . »

***

Fossi stato più frivolo, amico . . .
L'inverno si rifà salute,
lascia il maestro, ci aspettano
tutti i paesi del mondo
e nessun ruolo.
Per chi avrà fiducia,
depongo lo stemma dell'invalido,
la foto dell'atleta e un mazzo di santini.
Ho tutti i treni che partono
e molte virtù.
Non credo più nell'opera
queste carte salutano.

I saw the belltower and the soaked stairway
from the village. I could be there
in the first row, in just a flash.
But the heart of the word
melts down and poisons me.
Better the loitering customer
who gets up and laughs:
 "Another man will flourish"—so he thinks—
"I won't go flying down
into the sultriness, into the dead shadow,
into the caves at the bottom of the valley."

***

I might have been more frivolous, my friend . . .
The winter recovers its health,
the master goes away, all of the countries
of the world are waiting for us
and no part to play.
For whoever will have confidence,
I lay down the invalid's coat of arms,
the athlete's photo and a bunch of holy pictures.
I have all the departing trains
and many virtues.
I no longer believe in work
these papers send regards.

da POESIA DELLA FONTE (1993)

from POETRY OF THE SOURCE (1993)

Il sonno del mattino

La casa al mare

Non sono più nella mia casa,
ma in questa sede ariosa che mi concede tutto.
La sua tranquilla geometria
dà ingresso al chiaro per i corpi
umidi e leggeri sul terrazzo.
Ascolto di qui le voci della piazza,
osservo come un lago il mare che si apre
nel bosco e se c'è vento
una domestica campagna di cicale
che a mezzogiorno protegge i nostri passi.
Dipinta di azzurro e di bianco
la Brise Marine raccoglie gente che non ha
questi giardini riflessi negli occhi,
né le tracce feriali di una pigra incuria.
Mi affaccio distante per vedere
quei musi di pesce e la vernice
azzurra e viola che cola sulla pelle
di chi non sosta quando il tempo
non ha più direzione:
nella pianura totale, deserta,
e nel confine a taglio che si annebbia.

Morning Sleep

The House by the Sea

I'm not in my house anymore,
but in that breezy place that gives me everything.
Its serene geometry
provides an entryway to the light
for the damp and slender bodies on the terrace.
I hear from here the voices in the square,
I see the sea that opens like a lake
on the woods and if there is a wind
a domesticated countryside of cicadas
that shields our steps in the middle of the day.
Painted blue and white
the Brise Marine gathers people who
don't have these gardens reflected in their eyes,
or the weekday tracks of a lazy negligence.
I look into the distance to make out
the noses of the fish and the violet
and blue glaze dripping on the skin of those
who don't pause to rest when time
no longer has a direction:
across the entire plain, deserted now,
and at the clearing's edge where the fog rolls in.

Cecità della materia

Medusa marina corteccia
di dentro abitata da mille creature
come le forme dell'animazione
e quelle bocche nere dell'infanzia.
Materia senza occhi ma vivente
che rigermina in attimi infiniti
e lascia tracce viola sulla roccia
della sua casa notturna.

Blindness of Matter

Marine medusa shell
inhabited within by a thousand creatures
like forms of animation
and those black mouths of infancy.
Matter that has no eyes but is alive
regerminating in instants without end
and leaving violet traces on the rock
of its nocturnal home.

L'ospite bilanciato

da Chagall a Velázquez

Prima persona o terza ben confuse
e le due teste sovrapposte ai vetri verdi:
le due figure sono forse una.
Disteso lunghissimo di legno
il capo nell'erba, il cappello caduto
nel verde spalmato, bagnato,
il pino, il cielo lilla e il tetto dell'infanzia,
le braccia al cuore a croce,
lo steccato:
ma forse è un pretesto di narciso.

Di casa eppure estraneo,
provvisorio e centrale aspirato
in un risucchio di luce
dietro la piccola folla delle damigelle,
i sovrani, il cane, i nani,
l'artefice, l'ospite bilanciato.
Eccomi, sono lui,
i piedi sui gradini
della porta a un passo
dalla luce bianca del mondo
che c'è fuori.

The Balanced Guest

from Chagall to Velázquez

First and third persons thoroughly confused
and the two heads superimposed on the green glass:
the two figures might be one.
Endlessly stretched out and wooden
the head in the grass, the hat fallen down
in the smeared wet greenery,
the pine tree, lilac sky, and roof of childhood,
the arms crossed over the heart,
the fence:
but, it might be, a pretext for narcissus.

At home and yet a stranger
provisional and central aspirated
in an eddy of light
behind the little crowd of damoiselles,
the dynasts, the dog, the dwarves,
the artificer, the balanced guest.
Here I am, I am he,
feet on the steps
of the door a step away
from the white light of the world
that waits outside.

Divano

Un divano accostato alla parete:
sì, più provvisorio, improprio, esposto
e quasi miserabile
per questo polveroso eroe
che sogna un letto di piume
dove incurvarsi prima di affondare
protetto da un vecchio nella stanza
che russa dolcemente
serio e supino,
mentre già penetra dalle gelosie
il primo annuncio del mattino.

Couch

A couch pressed up against the wall:
yes, most provisional, inappropriate, exposed
and almost paltry
for this dusty hero
who dreams of a featherbed
fit for curling up in before sinking
shielded by an old man in the room
who's softly snoring
serious and supine,
while the first annunciation of the morning
already penetrates from the Venetian blinds.

Sonno del mattino

Nel sonno del mattino
sfuma il rimorso e l'abbandono
genera quasi dei prodigi.

Ma la notte è ancora combattuta
e all'alba s'impregna di sporcizia.

Poi si ricuce
nel primo oziare della luce,
e tra la gente delle vie qui intorno,
come una specie di allegria.

Morning Sleep

In morning sleep
remorse evaporates and letting go
generates near wonders.

And yet the night's still troubled and
at dawn you're soaked with grunge.

Then you mend
in the first luxuriating of the light,
and in the crowds in the streets hereabouts,
like a kind of buoyancy.

Vecchiaie

Oggi che troppe vecchiaie opprimono
così vicine, qualcosa si proietta
oltre la doppia porta, oltre le scale,
il cortile verde cupo e il portone
nell'indefinibile terra
dove quello che non è stato
andrà a comporsi
nella camera quieta e senza colpe
delle morti oneste.

Old People

Today with too many old people oppressing
so close around, something is projected
beyond the double doors, beyond the stairs,
the dark green courtyard and the outer gate
into the enigmatic earth
where what was not will go
to be composed
inside the silent and the guiltless chamber
of the honest dead.

Il sogno di Oblomov

Sul divano
c'era un asciugamano dimenticato
e la pipa abbandonata.

Dove siamo?

È una mattina bellissima . . . La casa,
gli alberi, la colombaia. Tutto
viene a gettare un'ombra lunga.
Il bambino diventa pensieroso
mentre si guarda attorno
e abbraccia ogni cosa, gli adulti
che si danno da fare nel cortile.

Ecco, si sentono dei passi,
uno si copre il viso con il fazzoletto,
poi si getta a terra e va a sdraiarsi
sotto un cespuglio.

Anche lui parla,
con una voce che non sembra sua.

Oblomov's Dream

On the sofa
there was a forgotten towel
and the abandoned pipe.

Where are we?

It's a glorious morning . . . The house,
the trees, the dovecote. Everything
starts casting a long shadow.
The little boy grows thoughtful
as he looks around him
and takes it all in, the adults
busying themselves in the courtyard.

Here, footsteps are heard,
one covers up his face with a handkerchief,
then drops down on the ground and stretches out
under a bush.

He speaks too,
in a voice that doesn't seem to be his own.

Quasi una tecnica

Mese dopo mese
giace nell'alto della luce
e nella notte fisica della sua mente.
« Raffigurare i piedi, le barbe,
i muri, il pane, i tavoli
in un oggetto sacro »,
ecco il pensiero mentre usciva
dal fianco mettendosi calato
sulla schiena a vedere l'ora
come in ospedale.
« Faccio una vita anonima
e credo che sia un bene »,
sorrideva tornando
e tutto il corpo rispondeva veloce
verso il basso e il buio,
seguito da un languore consolato.

Almost a Method

Month after month
he lies in the summit of the light
and in the physical night of his mind.
"To depict the feet, the beards,
the walls, the bread, the tables
in a sacred object,"
so he was thinking as he moved off
his side and put himself down
on his back to see the time
as in a hospital.
"I create an anonymous life
and I think it's a good thing,"
he smiled as he turned back
and his whole body swiftly responded
to the darkness and the depth,
followed by a comforting listlessness.

Davanzale

Fra il tetto e il davanzale, nel cortile,
quelle bestie malate, quando è ancora buio,
gemono, urlano in un coro altissimo.
Penetrano, lugubri, attraverso i vetri,
nei rantoli, nei sussulti animali,
nell'odore e negli occhi chiusi della stanza.
Sono con noi.

Windowsill

Between the roof and the windowsill, in the courtyard,
those ailing creatures, while it is still dark,
are moaning, howling in a piercing chorus.
Mournfully, they penetrate the windows
in their rasping, in their animal tremors,
in their smell and in the closed eyes of the room.
They are with us.

Letto

Qua sotto fiatiamo caldi
buone bestie tenere

Oh come siamo dolci e inermi,
buoni e sospesi nell'oblìo del giorno,
nelle piume e nel poco
che ci protegge scarmigliati,
gli occhi socchiusi, e gli sguardi si sfiorano
in un tocco per sempre che ci fa comuni,
quaggiù depositati, stirandoci a grattarci
nel caldo inverno dei colori.

Bed

> *Down here we breathe warmly*
> *nice tender beasts*

Oh how soft and defenseless we are, so nice
and suspended in the oblivion of the day,
in feathers and in the faint
protection of our disheveled selves,
our eyes half-shut, and our glances graze each other
in an endless touch that binds us up together,
deposited down here, stretching to scratch ourselves
in this warm winter full of colors.

Balcone

Seduto come un vecchio sul balcone
guardavo con invidia le volate
e poi le ricopiavo sul pavimento rosso.
Lei, forse offesa per la mia luna, mi diceva:
« Non c'è la mamma, ma è per poco.
Sembra che qui sei sulle spine,
ma perché? »

Perché c'è un arco chiaro, un'ala enorme
che ci tocca dentro, e io divento
quest'abulia sospesa e questo guscio
pieno di fessure.

Balcony

Sitting on the balcony like an old man
I enviously watched the flights and then
I imitated them on the red floor.
Maybe annoyed by my mood, she said to me:
"Mama's not here, but it's just for a little while.
You seem to be on pins and needles here,
but why?"

Because there's a clear arc, an enormous wing
that touches us within, and I'm turning into
this suspended abulia and this shell
full of cracks.

'53

L'uomo era ancora giovane e indossava
un soprabito grigio molto fine.
Teneva la mano di un bambino
silenzioso e felice.
Il campo era la quiete e l'avventura,
c'erano il kamikaze,
il Nacka, l'apolide e Veleno.
Era la primavera del '53,
l'inizio della mia memoria.
Luigi Cucchi
era l'immenso orgoglio del mio cuore,
ma forse lui non lo sapeva.

'53

The man was still young and he had on
a very fine gray overcoat.
He was holding the hand of a quiet
and happy little boy.
The field was stillness and it was adventure,
there they were, the Kamikaze,
Nacka, the man without a country, Poison.
It was the spring of '53,
the beginning of my memory.
Luigi Cucchi
was the huge pride and joy of my heart,
but maybe he didn't know it.

Valeria

Una gaiezza che somigliava
a una malinconia gentile
e nella veste rosa, e nel dolore,
un incedere solenne, delicato
per i corridoi. E poi
che tenerezza in grembo,
com'era ansiosa la periferia . . .

C'era qualcuno che sgusciava
ogni momento con il suo ditino,
tra porte, portieri e ascensori,
vetrate, cuffie e camici,
a portarti il suo semplice messaggio,
per sempre, di appartenenza.

Valeria

A gaiety that resembled
a gentle melancholy,
and dressed in pink, and in pain,
a delicate, solemn advance
through the corridors. And then
such tenderness at her breast,
how anxious were the outskirts . . .

There was someone who slipped away
every moment with his little finger,
between doors, doormen and elevators,
glass doors, caps and lab coats,
to bring you his simple message,
forever, of belonging.

Il canto del silenzio

Il mite fanciullo franato
storpiava urlando nei denti storti
il canto del silenzio.
Forse, come annotava il consigliere,
nel suo torpore era troppo spesso
rannicchiato.

Vorrei che qui, sotto il canto, le voci,
si udisse il disturbo dei passi,
lo sbattere di porte e della tosse,
lo strusciare
di vesti e piedi che si muovono dai banchi
verso la balaustra. Tra le campane
e le voci degli officianti,
tutto una cosa sola.

The Song of Silence

The gentle boy who'd collapsed
was mangling, howling through his crooked teeth,
the song of silence.
Maybe, as the counselor had noted,
he was too often huddled over
in his lethargy.

I wish that here, under the song, the voices,
you could hear the commotion of the footsteps,
the banging of the doors and all the coughing,
the rustling
of clothing and feet moving away from pews
toward the railing. Between the bells
and the voices of the celebrants,
all one single thing.

Vetrina

La vetrina del perito Barawitzka
era all'ingresso del borgo raggrumato,
anima opaca e personale di Milano.
Lambrate, come Niguarda,
dov'ero stato fortunato.

Ma il borgo della mente è fonte fissa,
muri di via Varé, di via Candiani,
tra le pozzanghere, i cortili e l'officina
di Luigi Cucchi.
Via Verità, e la desolazione
onirica del borgo, orgoglio,
verità senza bellezza
che espone all'orizzonte la sua sottostoria
in un recinto fradicio,
in un altrove ovunque
non degno di memoria: impassibile,
senza pietà.

Shop Window

The shop window of the surveyor Barawitzka
was at the entrance of the clotted district,
the opaque and personal essence of Milan.
Lambrate, like Niguarda,
where I'd been happy.

But the district of the mind is a fixed source,
the walls of Via Varé, of Via Candiani,
amid the puddles, the courtyards and the workshop
of Luigi Cucchi.
Via Verità, and the oneiric
desolation of the district, pride,
truth without beauty
exposing its understory to the horizon
in a putrid enclosure,
in an elsewhere nowhere
worth remembering: impassive,
pitiless.

Gorée

L'isola di Gorée guarisce
l'ansia del non ritorno.

Dalla scialuppa pensava alla vetrina
dell'istituto, spiava spalle e occhi,
i corpi così nobili.
La casa degli schiavi
aperta sull'oceano da una buca,
il verde polveroso e basso come a Mozia
e il cannone sulla cima.
Il piccolo albergo rosso, feriale,
per una birra. La sabbia quieta,
come nella cartolina, e i ragazzi
sdraiati al sole di dicembre.

Così imprevista e mite
e delicata l'Africa.

Gorée

The island of Gorée cures
the anxiety of not returning.

From the longboat he thought about the glass case
in the institute, he watched the backs and eyes,
such stately bodies.
The House of Slaves
open to the ocean through a hole,
the greenery low and dusty as at Mozia
and the cannon at the summit.
The ordinary little red hotel
for a beer. The placid sand,
just as on the postcard, and the boys
lying stretched out in the December sun.

So unexpected and mild
and delicate, Africa.

Incendio

L'incendio era un rettangolo rosso, e bucava la costa a un centimetro dal mare.

Poi quel mattino, verso la cima, come sospeso in un salto nella nube, l'amico alzando un po' le spalle mi avvertiva col suo sorriso acuto e complice: « Si avvicina, scendiamo tutti al porto ».

Io osservavo il suo abito nocciola.

Dal finestrino aperto sulla campagna vedevo l'ombrellone e le sedie del nostro mezzogiorno, sentivo il fumo, respiravo cenere.

Lasciavamo la casa senza nemmeno un saluto.

Sul pontile alcune donne si sbracciavano ridendo, facendo cadere quegli stracci colorati. « Meno male . . . », diceva il mio amico fregandosi le mani.

Nel cassone metallico il sonno è sui sedili. Umido, tra la cuffia e la coperta, il film e i soliti treni che perdevano la strada. Senza sapere più se partivo o tornavo, irrimediabilmente perso nella lontananza.

Fire

The fire was a red rectangle, and it cut a hole in the coast down to a centimeter from the sea.

Later that morning, toward the summit, as if suspended in a leap in the haze, shrugging his shoulders slightly my friend warned me with his sharp and knowing smile: "It's coming closer, let's all go down to the harbor."

I noticed his nut-brown suit.

Through the window that opened out on the countryside I saw the beach umbrella and the chairs that we used in the afternoon, I smelled the smoke, I breathed the ash.

We left the house without even saying goodbye.

On the pier a few women were waving their arms and laughing, letting their colorful rags fall. "Thank goodness . . . ," my friend said, rubbing his hands.

In the metal cassone the sleeping is on seats. Damp, between the headset and the blanket, the film and the usual trains losing their way. Without knowing any longer whether I was coming or going, hopelessly lost in the distance.

Lettere di Carlo Michelstaedter

Vi siete accorti, dal modo come scrivo,
che ho molto sonno . . .
Però non mi lasciate senza lettere,
scrivetemi, vi supplico . . .
Sarò calmo e normale,
ma che angoscia il distacco, non è vero?
E tu, mamma, non puoi non essere contenta:
sono con tutti allegro, sempre,
sono stato sincero con voi,
sono sempre lo stesso . . .
Ma le strade hanno in fondo
come una nebbia dorata e gli occhi
non vedevano che buio da ogni parte . . .
È un incubo d'inerzia faticosa,
l'inerzia nemica delle cose . . .
Il porto è la furia del mare.
Vi bacio, miei stronzetti adorati.

Letters of Carlo Michelstaedter

You will have noticed, from the way I write,
that I am very sleepy . . .
But please don't leave me here without a letter,
write to me, I beg you . . .
I'll be calm and normal,
though parting is such anguish, isn't it?
And you, mama, you cannot but be pleased:
I'm cheerful with everyone, always,
I've been honest with you,
I'm always the same . . .
But the far ends of the avenues
seem to be like a gilded mist and my eyes
saw nothing but the dark on every side . . .
It's a nightmare of wearying inertia,
inertia inimical to things . . .
The port is the fury of the sea.
I kiss you, my beloved little shits.

Risveglio

Eccolo uscire dalla pasta
maleodorante del suo sonno
barcollando nella nausea
già alto il sole,
strusciare la pelle tra gli spigoli
fino al richiamo che si apre
verso la strada, il pino e il mare.
Incerto, abbagliato scorge in basso
le donne distese e un omino
dai riccioli biondi sorridere,
dire qualcosa e andare via veloce.

Qui si scioglie l'accidia in uno slancio,
come in un gesto alato,
e va planante oltre l'appoggio,
nell'aria tiepida e nei corpi,
o forse nello stacco a precipizio
e nella bocca aperta della luce.

Waking

Here he is getting up and moving
away from the foul-smelling paste of his sleep
staggering around in nausea
the sun already high,
skin rubbing up against all the rough edges
all the way to the lure that opens out
toward the street, the pine tree and the sea.
Dazzled and unsteady, he makes out
the women stretched out down below
and a smiling little man with golden curls
saying something and hurrying away.

Here indolence is melted in a rush,
as in a winged gesture,
and it goes gliding past the balustrade,
into the tepid air and into the bodies,
or else perhaps into a sudden takeoff
and into the wide open mouth of the light.

Poesia della fonte

Salire e infossare lo sguardo:
nel cupo ci dev'essere un punto geometrico,
fra questi blocchi di pietra
e questa spaccatura e ogni volta
appare, sgorga, va e allora è
come se fosse incessantemente
nel chiuso della valle.

***

Sul tetto di roccia strapiombano
le rovine dell'ospite.
Io mi incammino tra i passeggeri e i vigili
in nulla differente di visibile.
Però cerco una fonte che sia solo mia.

***

Qui parlo per me
senza schermo o figura
e mi basto com'ero:
questa sola radice ricoperta di terra.

***

Poetry of the Source

To ascend and to bury the gaze:
in the dark there must be a geometric point,
between these blocks of stone
and this fissure and every time
it appears, it flows, it goes and then
it is as if it were unceasingly
in the enclosure of the valley.

***

The ruins of the host overhang
the rock roof.
I set forth among travelers and the vigilant
not visibly different in any way.
Yet I'm looking for a source that is mine alone.

***

Here I speak for myself
without a screen or figure
and I'm content to be what I was:
this single root that's covered up with earth.

***

Forse la fonte è una frase,
una domanda spaccata, una figura
che copre un'altra figura
e un'altra ancora.
Ma non all'infinito.

***

Infine venga al sole sgominando
tra due attimi altissimi.
I miei volti abolisca,
luce nella luce.

***

Ho bussato per la seconda volta
alla piccola casa del poeta.
Alle spalle un verde senza roccia,
acque rimaste dolci
e quasi una pianura.
Mi respinge, pensavo,
per non averlo abbastanza amato.

Nell'imbrunire tornavo a crogliolarmi
e la mia luna era l'elogio dell'oblìo.

Maybe the source is a phrase,
a broken question, a figure
that covers another figure
and yet another.
But not without end.

***

Let it come to the sun scattering in the end
between two towering instants.
Let it annul my faces,
light within light.

***

I've knocked for the second time
at the poet's little house.
Behind me a rockless green,
waters still sweet
and almost a plain.
He's rejecting me, I thought,
for not having loved him enough.

Then I returned to bask in the growing dark
and my moon was the eulogy of oblivion.

Al Cairo

Le case degli operai
avevano cortili a sassi
che davano in altri cortili.
Penso al foppone della peste,
osservo il giallo della Polveriera
e ti aspetto qui fuori,
al Cairo, tra le bisce del portone.

***

Il console generale a Bogotà
aveva annotato, grazioso,
che nei sobborghi di Milano
c'erano certi casoni . . .
E cento stanze cento famiglie, e i bimbi
erano rossi e allegri,
moltissimi, e bellissimi.

Ma a giudicare dalla famosa foto,
di settant'anni dopo,
e che tu chiami dei bambini esposti,
il nobile di Zenevredo,
l'eccellente scrittore si sbagliava.

***

At the Cairo

The houses of the workers
had courtyards paved with stones
that gave onto other courtyards.
I think of the cemetery for the plague,
I notice the yellow of the Polveriera
and I wait for you here outside,
at the Cairo, between the snakes of the main entrance.

***

The consul general at Bogotà
had charmingly noted that
in the suburbs of Milan there were
certain blocks of apartment buildings . . .
And a hundred units a hundred families, and the babies
were ruddy and merry,
plentiful, and adorable.

But judging by that famous photograph
from seventy years ago,
and the fact that you call some of the babies foundlings,
the nobleman from Zenevredo,
the excellent writer seems to have been mistaken.

***

E siano per sempre benedetti
i nostri cuori senza nome.
Guardo le ossa a croce della Schola
gratto le carte dell'Ornato fabbriche
fiutando un muso di padrone,
le sue pareti di polvere.
E c'era una nonnina *bogianen*,
le rughe nere un ghigno e il cappellino,
forse venuta dalla Portascia delle uova
a un passo dal giardino dei pavoni.
Lei conosceva lo stradone di Loreto,
il pullulare e l'umido, le scale
e la stanzetta di mia madre
la mia finestra di bambino.

***

« La tua maglietta rossa sarà la più bella,
e con un simbolo chiaro, proprio qui sul petto. »

Lo diceva il giovane dal braccio ferito,
e lui capiva e non capiva.
Sarà stato il '50, il '51,
gli parlava della corsa dei fiori,
la Milano Sanremo.

« Dopo l'ultimo scatto, e passata la fontana,
sorriderai nella vittoria dei colori giusti,
e avrai le braccia alzate del campione. »

***

And may they be forever blessed,
our nameless hearts.
I gaze upon the crossed bones of the Schola
I scratch the Old Buildings Commission's papers
catching a whiff of a landlord's mug,
its walls of dust.
And there was a pigheaded little old granny
dark wrinkles and a sneer and the little bonnet,
maybe come from the Portascia with eggs
just a few steps away from the peacock garden.
She was familiar with the Loreto road,
the swarming and the dampness, the stairway
and my mother's little room
my window when I was small.

***

"Your red T-shirt will be the best-looking one,
and with a clear emblem, right here on the chest."

The young fellow with the injured arm told him so,
and he understood and didn't understand.
This would have been in '50, '51,
and he was talking about the race of the flowers,
the Milan–San Remo.

"After the last sprint, when they've passed the fountain,
you'll be smiling when the right colors win,
and you'll be holding the champion's arms up high."

***

Il viaggiatore di città
va ozioso per le vie in ore di lavoro.
Accarrezza un istante la muraglia delle case,
osserva balconi, ruggini e si intrufola
tra le portinerie e i depositi.
Si crede indifferente, estraneo,
ma qualche volta lo prende la memoria,
lo turba un sentimento dissepolto.
Ma poi c'è sempre, a un ultimo piano,
una ragazza inquieta, che scosta una tendina.

***

L'uomo della Bovisa non poteva immaginare
che il suo avvenire, così presto,
sarebbe diventato preistoria.
Torna e rimugina quei nomi: la Società Smeriglio,
l'Officina del Gas e scopre come un monumento
la torre di mattoni altissima,
dove di dentro gli operai si arrampicavano.

In un oblìo forse sognante, quei diroccamenti
e le navate al sole o nella palta,
gli immensi alberi strani contro il cielo, nelle refezioni,
gli insegnano la muta dignità delle rovine.

***

The wanderer in the city
idles through streets in the middle of the workday.
He strokes the walls of the houses for a moment,
he looks at balconies, rust, and pokes around
the janitor's quarters and the storage rooms.
He thinks he's an outsider, uninvolved,
but memory takes hold of him sometimes,
a disinterred feeling comes to trouble him.
But there is always, up on a top floor,
a restless girl, pulling a curtain aside.

***

Never could the man from Bovisa have
imagined that his future would so quickly
be turned into an ancient history.
He returns and ponders those names: the Emery Company,
the Gasworks, and he sees like a monument
the dazzlingly high brick tower
in whose inside the workers used to clamber.

In a possibly dreamy forgetfulness, those dismantlings
and the naves in sunlight or in mud,
the strange enormous trees against the sky, during school lunches,
teach him the silent dignity of ruins.

***

La casa dei lavandai
offre con calma il suo trapasso,
scivola e gronda nella Martesana,
vicino agli orti luridi,
alle strutture afone e a un bambino
che si incammina quieto nella melma.

Il viaggiatore torna curioso sui suoi passi,
tra i padiglioni che fluttuano ingabbiati,
obliqui, semisommersi dalle alghe.
Pensa a una tinozza di piume e di calore,
tira su il bavero e riflette
su queste transizioni.

The house of the laundrymen
patiently offers up its passing away,
slides and drips into the Martesana,
near the filthy kitchen gardens,
to the soundless structures and a little child
who's making his way tranquilly through the muck.

The wanderer curiously turns back on his footsteps,
amid the pavilions floating caged,
slanting, half-submerged with algae.
He thinks of a tub of feathers and of heat,
tugs on his collar and reflects
on these transitions.

L'ULTIMO VIAGGIO DI GLENN (1999)

GLENN'S LAST JOURNEY (1999)

Rutebeuf

Rutebeuf passeggiava come un santo,
guardava la facciata delle case
come ripida roccia friabile.

***

Così mi chiamo
perché il mio nome
viene da *rude*, e *bue*.

***

Era impeccabile
nel suo vestito chiarissimo di lino
quel poco appena liso e un boccolo brillante
gli ornava la fronte corrugata.

***

Povera testa e povera memoria
mi ha dato dio re della gloria
eppure non ho fiele né veleno.

***

Rutebeuf

Rutebeuf went walking like a saint,
he regarded the façades of all the houses
as steep and crumbly rock.

***

I am so called
because my name
comes from *rude*, and *beef*.

***

He was impeccable
dressed in his suit woven from brightest linen
that barely threadbare one and one shining curl
was the adornment of his furrowed brow.

***

God the king of glory gave to me
a poor head and a poor memory
and yet I'm lacking in both bile and venom.

***

Così mi verso nel niente,
scorro via nelle strade e nei mercati
come piscia di cane.

***

Sono ridotto in società
ma non ho più committenti.
Ho amici Jean Bodel e Baude Fastoul,
che furono i poeti lebbrosi.

***

Il pensiero come lampo d'istante
che comunica con l'infinito
e degenera nella parola.
La prosa è infida: nasconde
confini traboccanti d'insignificanza.

***

Perché portiamo addosso
questa materia cotta
o questa roba da macelleria?

***

So I spill out into nothingness,
I flow away in the streets and in the markets
like dog piss.

***

Now I've come down in society
but I have no more customers.
I have as friends Jean Bodel and Baude Fastoul,
who were the leper poets.

***

Thought like the flash of an instant
that communicates with the infinite
and degenerates into the word.
Prose is unfaithful: it conceals
borders that overflow with insignificance.

***

Why do we carry on our backs
this baked material
or this stuff from the butcher shop?

***

Indossa un camicione che gli arriva
ai piedi nudi. È piccolo
come un fanciullo, e ha le dita
intrecciate sul petto,
quasi in preghiera.
Con la sua faccia tonta
e il naso trilobato
mi dà un'idea di mitezza sognante
e di una nobiltà interiore un po' animale.
Per molto tempo ho guardato la figura
e ho riso.
Ora non più.

***

Il capitano Genestas
incontra il vecchio cretino morente:
è il loro ultimo idolo.
Ma dove questi esseri vivono
la gente crede che portino fortuna alla famiglia.
In certe valli dove abbondano
vivono all'aria aperta con le greggi.

***

All'alba sono ancora al primo sonno
e ho fatto il sogno
di questa povera pietanza.

***

He's wearing a shirt that reaches all the way
to his bare feet. He's small
just like a little boy, and has his fingers
intertwined across his breast,
almost as if he's praying.
With his dopey face
and his trilobar nose
he gives me the notion of a dreamy mildness
and an inner nobility a bit like an animal's.
For a long time I used look at his figure
and I'd laugh.
Not anymore.

***

Captain Genestas
comes across the old dying idiot:
he is the last of their idols.
But in the places where these creatures live
people believe they bring the family good luck.
In certain valleys where they're plentiful
they live out in the open with the flocks.

***

At break of day I'm still in my first sleep
and I've had the dream
of this poor plate of food.

***

Il sole era già alto
e lei nella discesa oltre il cancello
così vecchina e piccola
infagottata nel suo cappotto blu.

Non potrò più dimenticare questi pomeriggi
seduto al tavolino col tuo vermut
a vederti mangiare

e dire: « In fondo la mia vita è stata povera,
ma non mi è mai mancato lo spirito ».

***

Ma anch'io, come la madre, godo del niente,
e se odio il sole che sorge
come lo vedo subito lo abbraccio.

***

Ci siamo lavati le mani per mangiare,
dietro di me siede la madre.

***

Tutto l'avvenire è già avvenuto.
E dove sono quelli che ho amato,
che accanto a me mi ero tenuto?
Gli amici sono spariti o sparsi:
il vento li ha portati via,
amici che il vento se li porta
e che soffiava davanti alla mia porta.

***

The sun was already high
and she going down the hill out past the gate
so old and small
bundled up in her blue coat.

I never can forget those afternoons
sitting at the coffee table with your vermouth
watching you eat

and say: "All in all I've had a wretched life,
but never have I been dispirited."

***

But, like my mother, I take pleasure in nothing,
and even though I despise the rising sun
the moment that I see it I embrace it.

***

We've washed our hands before eating,
my mother's sitting behind me.

***

All that will happen has already happened.
And now where are the ones that I have loved,
all of those that I held close to me?
My friends are scattered or have disappeared:
the wind has carried them away,
friends that the wind has carried off
and that it blew away before my door.

***

Solo questo so fare e non c'è altro,
e mi applico pigro, superbo, negligente,
e lo faccio anche male.

***

Il maestro era il mio caro amico
e io gli avevo dato, nella mia mente,
decoro di nuovo padre, tanto che lui,
ancora dopo, ancora adesso,
veniva e viene a visitarmi in sogno.

***

Nella casa della nostra giovinezza
oltre il lavandino,
strofinavo le mani macchiate di vino
sulla pietra del davanzale,
mentre usciva dalla mezza vasca
un odore di marcio.

***

Strofinava i risvolti e i polpastrelli
sul ruvido dei muri,
come per lasciare un brandello impresso
una macchia di sé, d'inchiostro.

***

This is all I know how to do and there's nothing else,
and I go at it lazily, haughtily, negligently,
and I do it badly too.

***

The master was a very dear friend of mine
and I had given to him, in my mind,
the honor of a new father, so much so
that even after, even now,
he came and comes to visit me in dreams.

***

In the house where we grew up
beyond the sink,
I rubbed my wine-spotted hands
on the stone of the windowsill,
while from the little basin there arose
an odor of rot.

***

He rubbed his cuffs and his fingertips
on the roughness of the walls,
as if to leave a shred imprinted
a spot of himself, an inkblot.

***

Trovandomi alla finestra d'un cavalcavia,
vidi un uomo con una carta in mano,
sopra la quale pareva che scrivesse,
poi si fece vicino alla muraglia delle case
e vidi che l'attaccava con le mani.

***

Vedevo nella stanza buia
tutte le luci del firmamento.
Il tuono mi faceva galleggiare
in squarci di vertigine e terrore
davanti all'orizzonte del mio vuoto.

***

E il colpo si era diffuso
nella testa del mio povero padre
e gli aveva spaccato la testa.

***

Non c'era bisogno di tanta violenza,
mi dicevi. Dio inverecondo
che maneggi le cause e non ti fai vedere
non farle più del male.

***

Nell'asfalto viscido del film,
la mano del pugile schiacciata da un mattone.

***

Finding myself at the window of an overpass,
I saw a man with a paper in his hand,
and it seemed that he was writing something on it,
then he approached the wall around the houses
and I saw he was attacking it with his hands.

***

I saw in the dark room
all the lights of the firmament.
The thunder made me start to float
in slashes of vertigo and terror
before the horizon of my emptiness.

***

And the stroke was diffused
through my poor father's head
and his head was split.

***

There was no need for so much violence,
you told me. Shameless God
who fashions the causes and doesn't let you see
how not to make them worse.

***

On the asphalt oily with its film,
the boxer's hand crushed by a brick.

***

Tornando vedeva certe incisioni di Rosa.
L'uomo che indica e l'altro con una specie di turbante,
quei pochi ciuffi di barba,
un fascio di stracci lungo il corpo e i piedi.
Appoggiato a una picca, derelitto, diceva:
« Preferirei non essere soldato ».

**

Noi eravamo una casa nel mare
e adesso in terra si sono mossi i vermi.

**

Ho rotto il mio bicchiere,
tutti i bei giorni sono già passati.

**

E intanto le due donne
stavano guardando dove lo mettevano.

Returning he saw some of Rosa's engravings.
The pointing man and the one with a sort of turban,
those few tufts of beard,
a bundle of rags along the body and the feet.
Leaning on a pike, forlorn, he said:
"I would prefer not to be a soldier."

***

We were a house in the sea
and now the worms have moved into the earth.

***

I've broken my drinking glass,
all the good days have already passed.

***

And meanwhile the two women
were keeping vigil there where they had placed him.

Ragna

a Enrico Della Torre

Cerco nuovi percorsi
a minime distanze,
oltre le solite muraglie.
Percorsi sottili di ragna
nel piano paziente e leggero
che solo a fili pare che s'intrichi.

Infiorescenze, terra,
pulizia intatta.
Qualcuno fa i suoi passi,
si allontana,
eppure è sempre lì.

***

Siamo figure indistinte
e così indissolubili
eppure senza tracce,
ormai senza volere.

E giri piano
verso la luce, il cilindro,
osservando figure mutanti,
geometrie, reticoli, tele.

Sentiamo un po' di vertigine
o il peso del buio nelle fibre.

***

Spiderweb

to Enrico Della Torre

I'm looking for new paths
at minimal distances,
beyond the usual walls.
Slender spiderweb paths
on the mild and patient plain
that merely seems tangled in threads.

Inflorescences, ground,
unbroken tidiness.
Somebody passes by,
he goes away,
and yet he's always there.

***

We're indistinct shapes,
thus indissoluble,
and yet without traces,
by now without will.

And you turn slowly
toward the light, the cylinder,
watching mutant shapes,
geometries, networks, webs.

We feel a little bit of dizziness
or the weight of darkness in our fibers.

***

La materia non è un'idea,
ma certe volte si riassume
in tracciati composti, in linee.
Ma è più che altro un'illusione
e nel suo trasparire
s'insinua il corpo scuro
di un'ala opaca, cupa,
che ci calca la fronte.

Poi in una primavera limpida,
senza riserve,
dopo o dentro il disastro,
vedi la gente passare
e il gioco veloce degli occhi
ti invoglia ancora a strofinare
i grumi delle facciate.

***

Da questa zona bassa e vacillante,
non so se il monte mi porterà in alto,
o verrà a imprimermi
come un residuo fossile schiacciato,
strozzato in gola.
               Ma sogno
lo spaccamento del sasso
e che non sia asciutto,
e si sprigioni.
Anche se il fiume scorre sempre,
ma noi no.

***

Matter is not an idea,
but it abstracts itself at times
into composed outlines, into lines.
But it's mostly an illusion
that in its shining
creeps into the dark body
of a dull somber wing
pressing on our brows.

Then in a limpid absolute
springtime,
after or in the disaster,
you see the people passing
and the rapid play of eyes
lures you once more to rub
the lumps of the façades.

***

From this low and wavering area,
I don't know if the mountain will carry me up,
or if it will come to imbed me
like a bit of flattened fossil residue,
choked in the gorge.
                        But I dream
the splitting of the rock
and that it isn't dry,
and gushes out.
Even though the river always flows,
we don't.

***

Calcando terra davanti al lavandino,
c'era una roccia fluida,
una madre o una sposa,
un albero davanti al mare,
nubi volanti . . .

Mi fermo in una stanza desolata
dove finisce il viaggio.
Sono all'Hotel Riviera,
tra i camion e le giostre,
osservo l'acqua piatta,
passa la scia dei canottieri.

Treading the ground in front of the sink,
there was a fluid rock,
a mother or a bride,
a tree in front of the sea,
flying clouds . . .

I come to a halt in a desolate room
where the journey ends.
I'm at the Hotel Riviera,
amid the trucks and carousels,
I'm watching the flat water,
the wake of the rowers passes by.

Bosco d'isola

Non sono più nella mia casa,
ma in questa sede ariosa che mi concede tutto.
La sua tranquilla geometria
dà ingresso al chiaro per i corpi
umidi e leggeri sul terrazzo
nelle tracce feriali di una pigra incuria.

Ascolto di qui le voci della piazza,
osservo come un lago il mare che si apre
nel bosco e se c'è vento
una domestica campagna di cicale
che a mezzogiorno protegge i nostri passi
quando il tempo non ha più direzione:

nella pianura totale, deserta,
e nel confine a taglio che si annebbia.

***

Fritz mi aveva detto un po' sfuggente
che c'era vita notturna sull'isola.
Pensavo a quei piccoli scoscendimenti,
e labirinti, a quei tronchi sottili, a un solitario
infognarsi nelle tenebre e gustare
l'ansia gratuita, lo smarrimento, i brividi,
la terra.

Island Forest

I'm not in my house anymore,
but in that breezy place that gives me everything.
Its serene geometry
provides an entryway to the light
for the damp and slender bodies on the terrace
in the weekday tracks of lazy negligence.

I hear from here the voices in the square,
I see the sea that opens like a lake
on the woods and if there is a wind
a domesticated countryside of cicadas
that shields our steps in the middle of the day
when time no longer has a direction:

across the entire plain, deserted now,
and at the clearing's edge where the fog rolls in.

***

Fritz had said to me, a little bit
evasively, there was night life on the island.
I thought about those little landslides there,
and labyrinths, those slender tree trunks, and a solitary
sinking into the mire in the darkness
and savoring groundless anxiety, being lost, the shivers,
the ground.

Ricorrevo a infantili immagini prealpine,
a ciclamini, all'umido, ai profumi,
per inoltrarmi anch'io
tra i bei sentieri coperti di notte.
Ma quei tipi che bussavano,
nelle ore buie di vento e temporale,
alla nostra casetta e ci svegliavano,
avevano misteri più modesti nelle scarpe
e così il folto li avrebbe masticati
oppure qualche biscia nel silenzio
con dolcezza li avrebbe accarezzati.

***

Siamo tutti individui distinti
come i sassi nell'acciottolato.

Sono un'ampolla, una vescica
e trasudo me del mio stesso essere.

***

La vacanza ci apre un dolce vuoto
di sospensione piena e alla partenza
ci agita e respira infinita.

Amo la gente del mese d'agosto,
che galleggia nell'aria
e nel tempo assopito.
Amo la folla anonima,
che esplora i viali quieta
e ride al mare in un caffè all'aperto.

I resorted to childhood prealpine images
of cyclamens, of damp, of fragrances,
to keep myself moving forward
among the fine paths covered up by night.
But those guys who came knocking,
in the dark hours of wind and thunderstorm,
on the door of our little cabin and woke us up,
had more modest mysteries in their shoes
and so they would have been chewed up by the brake
or else they would have found themselves caressed
tenderly in the silence by some snake.

***

We are all individuals as distinct
from one another as the cobblestones.

I am a blister, I am a bladder
and I ooze myself from my very being.

***

Vacation opens up for us a sweet
void of complete suspension and on setting off
it stirs us up and endlessly breathes free.

I love the people of the month of August
floating in the air
and in the drowsy weather.
I love the anonymous crowd
quietly exploring the promenades
and laughing by the sea in an open-air cafe.

Col cappellaccio in testa,
sono già qui che aspetto la corriera.
Mi volto sempre indietro,
negli occhi ho la salita,
ma intanto l'isola è sparita.

A beat-up old hat on my head,
I'm here already waiting for the bus.
I'm always turning round,
eyes always on the climb,
but the island's disappeared in the meantime.

L'ultimo viaggio di Glenn

La prima immagine è il Lago di Garda,
scavata in bianco e nero fino all'Ortles.

Sarò solo un bambino,
ma mio padre vive in eterno.

Dopo la Jugoslavia, nel luglio '41,
con firma fiorita
salutava la Magda.

***

a Mauro

Il paese era sparso sulla schiena del colle
e mi scorreva limpido negli occhi.
Nell'aria illogica di un sole svizzero
come la donna bidimensionale
in visone e scarpe di plastica
che aspettava il bambino a scuola.
« Non sento quasi niente — ho detto — .
Però ti fermi su, alla chiesa,
e lasci che io vada solo in mezzo al bosco:
per rispetto, almeno, per raccoglimento ».

***

Glenn's Last Journey

The earliest of the images is Lake Garda,
dredged up in black and white all the way to the Ortler.

I'll be just a little boy,
and yet my father lives eternally.

After Yugoslavia, in July '41,
he greeted Magda
with a flowery signature.

***

to Mauro

The countryside was strewn on the back of the hill
and it ran limpidly before my eyes.
In the illogical air of a Swiss sun
like the two-dimensional woman who
was wearing a mink and shoes made out of plastic
and waited for the little boy at school.
"I can barely feel a thing"—I said—
"but nonetheless you wait there, at the church,
and let me go alone into the middle of the woods:
out of respect, at least, out of consideration."

***

La sera a casa,
ho capito che il fango era lo stesso
già chiaro e secco sulle scarpe.
Nel folto, cercavo, chissà perché,
uno spiazzo. Seguivo un suono d'acqua.
La carta militare indica il confine,
il Monte Prato, località
Morti e l'Annunziata.
Forse da lì, nel pieno dell'amore,
forse già col bambino obbediente e selvatico,
le aveva fatto segno con la mano:
« Ecco, è la Svizzera ».
Poi le ha lasciato un pegno postumo,
tragico e delicato,
com'era lui.

***

I ragazzi in divisa sono stati gentili,
ma negli archivi non c'era neanche il nome
di un uomo che quarant'anni prima, in primavera,
aveva fatto la sua gita in moto
nei verdi colli demarcati.

***

Forse Bernasconi
era stato con lui telarista all'Olympia.
Un pranzo nel sole pacifico,
dolce attraverso i vetri.
A tavola c'era una brocca, o una saliera,
e lui, trasognato, toccandola,
gli aveva detto: « Ci fosse lei,

At home in the evening,
I realized the mud was just the same,
already light and dried out on my shoes.
In the thick brush I was trying, who knows why,
to find a clearing. I followed the sound of water.
It's all on the military map: the border,
Mount Prato, the localities
of Morti and L'Annunziata.
Maybe from there, in the fullness of his love,
maybe now with an obedient and unsociable child,
he'd made a sign to them with a wave of his hand:
"Look, it's Switzerland."
Later he'd left them a posthumous token,
delicate and tragic,
like himself.

***

The boys in their uniforms were very polite
but the archives didn't even have the name
of a man who in the springtime forty years ago
had gone on his ride through the green
demarcated hills.

***

Maybe Bernasconi
was a framebuilder at Olympia with him.
A lunch in the placid sunlight,
filtered gently through the windows.
On the table was a pitcher, or a saltshaker,
and he, lost in a daydream, touching it,
said to him: "If only she were here,

ama le cose fini ». E qui chinò la fronte
e rimase turbato.
Forse cercava in lui una speranza,
l'ultimo credito umano e materiale.

***

Con un sorriso si specchiava nel campione
che al Vigorelli, dopo i bombardamenti,
batteva il record di Archambaud.
« Avevo una maglia di lana a quattro tasche
e giravo su un ferro da americanista ».
Glenn era tornato dalla Russia
e aveva ancora il braccio fermo.
Coppi, che era soldato,
andava a insabbiarsi in Tunisia.

***

Giunsi come un sacco sanguinante,
dice Bestetti del 3° Bersaglieri.
Partimmo dal Garda il 24 luglio
col grande affetto della popolazione.
Le strade dei Carpazi, il fango, il fiume Bug.
Parole come la famosa katiuscia,
città come Dniepropetrovsk.
Con il morale sempre altissimo,
entrammo nella Russia Bianca.
Il 27 agosto, il duce
visitò i nostri reparti. A Capodanno,
una granata centrò l'isba
e ne fui martoriato in tutto il corpo.

***

she loves fine things." And here he bowed his head
and was upset.
Maybe in him he was looking for some hope,
the last material and human trust.

***

With a smile he modeled himself on the champion
who, at the Vigorelli velodrome,
after the bombings, broke Archambaud's record.
"I had a woolen jersey with four pockets
and I was riding an American scooter."
Glenn had come back from Russia
and still had a stiff arm.
Coppi, who was a soldier,
went off to be choked with sand in Tunisia.

***

I arrived like a bleeding sack,
says Bestetti of the 3rd Bersaglieri.
We marched from Garda on July 24
with great affection from the people there.
The Carpathian roads, the mud, the river Bug.
Words like the famous *Katyusha*,
cities like Dniepropetrovsk.
With our morale always at tiptop
we crossed into White Russia.
On August 27, Il Duce
visited our detachments. On New Year's Day,
a grenade scored a bull's-eye on the *izba*,
and there wasn't an inch of me it didn't torture.

***

Nell'accecante paesaggio,
con gli occhi vitrei cercavamo la pista
e l'orizzonte a bucare la bufera.
Eravamo assaliti da visioni fantastiche
e dall'angoscia dell'ignoto.
I morti erano incollati a terra dal gelo.

***

— *À qui ai-je l'honneur de parler?*
— *Au colonel Chabert.*
— *Lequel?*
— *Celui qui est mort à Eylau.*

***

Non c'era stata odissea nel ritorno.
Le schegge l'avevano ferito al braccio destro,
al gomito. E io sulle ginocchia accarezzavo
il disegno sfrangiato di una macchia di latte.
Pare che al colpo balzasse in piedi con un urlo
di gioia e sangue, e si vedesse con un braccio solo
ridere in piazza Duomo.
Però chissà che scossa nella schiena
quando fu l'ultimo a salire
sull'ultimo aereo militare.

***

In the blinding landscape,
with glassy eyes we tried to find the trail
and the horizon so we could drill a hole in the squall.
We were assaulted by fantastic visions
and by the anguish of the unknown.
The dead were stuck to the ground by the freezing cold.

***

— *À qui ai-je l'honneur de parler?*
— *Au colonel Chabert.*
— *Lequel?*
— *Celui qui est mort à Eylau.*

***

There was no odyssey in his homecoming.
The shrapnel had wounded him in the right arm,
at the elbow. And sitting on his lap
I would caress the frayed pattern of a milkstain.
When it hit he seems to have leaped to his feet with a shout
of joy and blood, and was seen waving just one arm
and laughing in the Piazza Duomo.
And yet who knows what tremors he felt in his back
when he was the last to climb
aboard the last warplane.

***

Dalle immagini dell'ospedale,
si afferma che la verità riduce,
ma che la forza tiene.
Glenn non ha più la faccia
da film americano.
È un ragazzo colpito. Però, tra gli altri inermi
di una generazione,
lo sguardo misterioso e assente,
ripete: « Sono centrale,
sono il figlio più amato ».

***

Girava per Lecco chiamandola,
le parlava orgoglioso degli eroici piumati.
Ma era delicato, e così remissivo,
nell'evidenza del suo amore.

***

Dal Cairo a Loreto
pochi passi abbracciati sul corso
e c'ero io nella pancia.
Erano incerti e si scambiavano sorrisi
più teneri che inquieti.
Il duce era già appeso,
ma verso piazza Argentina,
col chiasso e la folla in confusione,
gli disse: « Luigi,
torniamo in casa ».

***

From the images of the hospital,
we can assert that he cuts back the truth,
but that he keeps his strength.
Glenn no longer has a face
from an American movie.
He's a battered kid. Yet among a generation's
other defenseless ones,
his gaze mysterious and faraway,
he keeps repeating: "I'm central,
I'm the most beloved son."

***

He wandered round through Lecco calling her,
he spoke to her proudly of his plumed heroics.
But he was weak, and so he was submissive,
in the display of his love.

***

From the Cairo to Loreto
a few steps, hugging, on the avenue
and I was there in her belly.
They were hesitant and traded smiles
that were more tender than troubled.
Il Duce was already strung up,
but heading toward Piazza Argentina,
with all the uproar and the crowd in chaos,
she said to him: "Luigi,
let's go home."

***

Il socio era sprezzante e fanfarone.
L'officina era sotterranea,
e i soldi pacchi di cambiali.
Ci portava ogni tanto dall'oste
allampanato, con gli occhialini
di metallo, Amanda Binet,
sporgendo il busto dal bancone,
contava i soldi con le unghie
bordeaux e se lo sguardava,
se lo mangiava.

***

Ci regalò un benessere leggero,
il mare e solo noi.
« Il verde è Inverigo », mi diceva.
Vedo ancora le case nel pendio
con il cuore appagato.
Ma dopo i nomi, Rampoldi . . . Soffientini . . .
i libri erano bianchi.

***

Ero con lei vicino all'officina.
Nella vestaglia nera da lavoro,
andava piano, sull'altro marciapiede.
Si era chinato un po',
si era appoggiato al muro.
Voltandomi, dicevo: « Guarda, piange! »
Lei mi ha scrollato, poi ha tirato dritto.
« È ubriaco », mi ha detto.

***

His partner was disdainful and a braggart.
The workshop was below the street,
and the money bundles of promissory notes.
Every so often, sent by the cadaverous
landlord, with metal-framed
eyeglasses, Amanda Binet arrived,
with bosom thrusting from behind the counter
she counted out the money with maroon
fingernails: if she glanced at it,
she grabbed it.

***

He gave us a sense of lighthearted wellbeing,
the sea and us alone.
"The green is Inverigo," he said to me.
I still can see the houses on the hillside
with a contented heart.
But after the names, Rampoldi . . . Soffientini . . .
the books were blank.

***

I was with her not far from the workshop.
In the black coverall he wore at work,
he was walking slowly, on the other sidewalk.
He was bent a bit,
he was leaning against the wall.
Turning around, I told her: "Look, he's crying!"
She shrugged at me, and then moved straight ahead.
"He's drunk," she said.

***

Enorme sulle gelosie un'ombra mossa,
nella vergogna di un mattino in grembo:
« Perché tutto, così, accade
in me, e solo in me »,
io rumino.
Poi l'ansare dell'ombra e un gemito
strozzato mentre si alza il maglio
e piomba giù per fare i pezzi,
furioso, la terra piana
dove poggia i piedi,
l'uomo sospeso, l'operaio,
nell'eterno sudore del mattino.

***

A tavola
faceva gesti strani, assorto.
Faceva i conti nell'aria.
Forse per questo il giornale ha parlato
di cagionevole salute.
Ho pensato al disordine, alle multe,
alle marmitte Innocenti
a un anno dal miracolo.

Li sentiva venire da tutte le parti
vide la sua firma saltellare
e cercò di acchiapparla.

***

A moving shadow enormous on the shutters,
in the shyness of a morning on his lap:
"Because everything falls on me,
and on me alone,"
I ruminate.
Then the shadow breathing heavily and a choked
groan as the hammer rises high
and comes down hard to make the parts,
furious, the ground flat
where he rests his feet,
the man suspended, the workman,
in the morning's everlasting sweat.

***

At the table
he made peculiar gestures, preoccupied.
He made calculations in the air.
Maybe that was why the newspaper
talked about poor health.
I thought about disorder, about fines,
about the Innocenti mufflers
in one year of the miracle.

He sensed them coming at him from all sides
he saw his signature jumping all around
and he tried to catch it.

***

Come un boato sorge quel canto:
Alleluja. La voce cieca
sale dalla terra immensa
e immensamente cavernosa:
Exultabuntur.

***

Stupefacente è la freddezza del disegno,
romantico, nella mortificazione, il compimento.
Forse aveva la mente spossata dall'inadempienza,
il cuore ferito dalla delusione
o gli martellava il braccio come un'eco di guerra,
nelle allucinazioni del mattino.

***

C'era un bel sole quel mattino di maggio.
Glenn se ne andava in moto dalla periferia,
la 6,35 in una tasca del vestito beige.
Vide l'amico nella casa al confine
e mangiò alla sua tavola
tranquillamente.
Tina era sempre golosa,
ecco perché il cercatore di funghi
che attraversava il bosco,
gli trovò addosso, trentasei ore dopo,
la tavoletta di cioccolato.

***

That chant ascends like a roar:
Alleluia. The blind voice
rises from the immense
and immensely cavernous earth:
Exultabuntur.

***

The coldness of the design is stupefying,
the execution romantic in its mortification.
Maybe his mind was exhausted from defaulting,
his heart was wounded by disappointment
or his arm tortured him like an echo of the war,
in the hallucinations of the morning.

***

The sun was shining bright on that May morning.
Glenn took off on his motorbike from the outskirts,
6:35 in a pocket of his beige suit.
He saw a friend of his at his house on the border
and sat at his table eating
peacefully.
Tina had always had a sweet tooth,
which is why the man who was walking through the woods
looking for mushrooms
found on him, thirty-six hours later,
a chocolate bar.

***

Glenn, come lo chiamavo nella mia mente io,
o com'è più dolce e semplice,
com'è più vero:
Luigi.
Resti per me una crepa d'affetto
o un lampo intermittente nel cervello.
E anche tu, che non l'hai mai visto,
lo ami.
Tu che hai taciuto, e oggi non taci più,
hai la memoria smangiata come la tua macula:
cerchi e non trovi più
nemmeno la sua voce.

***

Facevo il viale per arrivare al campo.
Attorno, uomini coi badili,
e io piangevo poco.
Ma davanti alla scatola col tuo vago sorriso,
bellissimo, con la camicia scura aperta
e il distintivo del ferito,
il gelo mi è venuto dentro.
« Cosa vuoi che ti dica? » ho fatto allora
con le mie rose in mano e con paura,
« forse è già il tempo dell'indifferenza ».
Forse sono decotto, forse io stesso
sono solo memoria di me stesso.

***

Glenn, as I have called him in my mind,
or as is sweeter and simpler,
as is truer:
Luigi.
To me you are still a crevice of affection
or an intermittent flashing in the brain.
And even you, you who never saw him,
love him.
You who were silent, and now are no longer silent,
your memory is as worn away as your macula:
you search and can no longer find
even his voice.

***

I took the avenue to get to the field.
All around, men with shovels,
and I wept a little.
But standing before the box with your vague smile,
so handsome, with your open dark shirt
and the badge of your wound,
I felt the chill come into me.
"What do you want me to tell you?" I said then
with my roses in my hand and a shiver of fear,
"maybe the time of indifference is here."
Maybe I'm bankrupt, maybe I myself
am nothing but a memory of myself.

***

Lui se ne andò gettandoci
nell'improvviso smarrimento.
In un sacchetto della polizia,
ecco gli assegni, il pettine,
la benda per il polso . . .

Ciao, dico adesso senza più tremare.
Io ti ho salvato, ascoltami.
Ti lascio il meglio del mio cuore
e con il bacio della gratitudine,
questa serenità commossa.

He went away throwing us
into sudden confusion and loss.
In a bag from the police,
there were checks, his comb,
his wrist bandage . . .

So long, I tell you now without trembling.
I've saved you, listen to me.
I leave you the best of my heart
and, with the kiss of gratitude,
this passionate serenity.

da PER UN SECONDO O UN SECOLO (2003)

from BY A SECOND OR A CENTURY (2003)

Malone non muore

Questa stanza è l'archetipo,
l'alloggio sordido e totale
che ambienta il film notturno.
Oltre il cortile si arriva
da una scala nera di pietra,
la luce dentro è scarsa, c'è il camino
e un sapore di tana nel tanfo.
Non so chi sia la donna che si spulcia,
né la vecchia che sale con la brocca
e dá un'occhiata al barbone col bambino.
Ma i fiaschi, le stoviglie, l'aglio appeso,
gli stracci, il cagnetto sul cuscino
danno un'idea di miseria e impostura
che vorrei riscattata in Emmaus,
col sacco e le pagnotte, le pupille
sgranate dell'uomo nella luce,
mentre laggiù una donna si affaccenda e lui,
buio signore sulla porta di travi,
non sai se è realtà o solo un'ombra.

***

Ho sempre pensato che la fine
è più importante dell'inizio
ma se la fine si versa nell'inizio
vengo fuori rifatto.

***

Malone Doesn't Die

This room is the archetype,
the squalid and complete accommodation
that's the setting for the nighttime movie.
Once you're past the courtyard you come in
by climbing a black staircase made of stone,
the room is dimly lit, there's a fireplace
and a taste of musty earth there in the air.
I don't know the woman picking fleas off herself,
or the old woman who gets up with the pitcher
and glances at the tramp with the little boy.
But the bottles, the crockery, the hanging garlic,
the rags, the puppy sitting on the pillow
give an idea of misery and deceit
that I would like to see redeemed at Emmaus,
with sackcloth and the loaves of bread, the pupils
of the man's eyes opened in the light,
while a woman bustles over there and he,
the dark gent in the timbered doorway, you don't know
if he's reality or just a shadow.

***

I've always thought that the end
is more important than the beginning
but if the end flows into the beginning
I come out remade.

***

Comunque sia non muoio subito, del tutto.
« Nascere è l'idea del momento »,
scrisse Malone con il suo mozzicone.

***

Amo strusciare il mio corpo
contro le pietre e l'erba
quando posso sgusciare
con gli occhi riaperti:
la palude animata, per fortuna,
è visibile a un passo
e questi cupi coperchi
s'incrinano di luce.

***

Ecco, ad esempio, numeri. Anni:
quarantacinque, cinquantasette,
settantuno, novantasette.
Misure: sette centimetri
dietro le coste, sette punti liquidi,
nell'occhio.
Anni sbagliati e calendari,
appuntamenti falliti
per un secondo o un secolo.

***

However it is, I don't die at once, all through.
"Being born, that's the brainwave now,"
so Malone wrote with his cigarette butt.

***

I love to rub my body
against rocks and grass
when I can slip off
with reopened eyes:
the lively marsh, luckily,
can be seen a few steps away
and these dark lids
are cracked by light.

***

Here are numbers, for example. Years:
forty-five, fifty-seven,
seventy-one, ninety-seven.
Measures: seven centimeters
behind the ribs, seven liquid pints,
in the eye.
Botched years and calendars,
appointments missed
by a second or a century.

***

Le parti più sensibili, più docili e reattive
in questo morbido piacere solitario
sono la bocca e il piede
che godono il contatto
passivo e ruvido del lattice, del lino,
sognando l'eterna piuma in un residuo
minimale di esperienza viva, ma capace
ancora di muovere un incontro,
nobile attrito nel corpo che giace.

***

La dimora era quasi
la cantina dei ciechi,
con molti allievi degli abissi. Flora,
biondina dolce come il falegname,
portava i livini del musicista di ringhiera,
e c'era Osvaldo dal labbro leporino.
In un ritaglio di foto, Icio ha un sorriso
accennato, sapiente, e porta un gilerino
a strisce, fatto in casa. Ma poi,
nelle sue bretelle di lana, alla vista del sole
sul laghetto tra i giardini e lo zoo,
sembrava volare come un uccellino
estasiato tra la gente, felice della primavera
e dei fiori, agitando le braccia. Eppure
era selvatico e solitario, propenso
a rannicchiarsi già allora nel torpore;
preciso e millimetrico nel gioco,
ma atterrito dalla compagnia.
« Questo bambino è un inetto
e non ha fantasia »,

The most sensitive, obedient and reactive parts
in this tender solitary pleasure
are the mouth and the foot
that enjoy the passive
and rough contact of the latex, of the linen,
dreaming the endless feather in a minimal
residue of living experience, but still
capable of provoking an encounter,
a noble friction in the reclining body.

***

The abode was practically
the cellar of the blind,
with many students of the depths. Flora,
blonde and gentle as a carpenter,
bore the bruises of the banister musician,
and Osvaldo with the harelip was there too.
In a piece cut out of a photograph, Icio
wears a hint of a knowing smile, and he has on
a homemade pinstriped vest. But then,
in his wool suspenders, in full view of the sun
on the pond between the gardens and the zoo,
he seemed to be flying around like an enraptured
little bird in the midst of the crowd, delighting in
the spring and the flowers, flapping his arms. And yet
he was wild and solitary, and already
inclined to curl up sluggishly back then;
precise and millimetric when he played
a game, but terrified by company.
"That boy's a good-for-nothing
and he has no imagination,"

sentenziò un giorno qualcuno
amato sopra ogni cosa,
e lui pensò che era vero.

***

Eppure ho varcato confini,
mi sono inoltrato con gioia e paura
verso terre ignote, città meravigliose.

someone he loved above all else
pronounced one day,
and he thought it was true.

***

Yet I've crossed borders,
have forged ahead in joy and apprehension
toward unknown lands and cities full of wonder.

Un'identità fittizia e un cervello prodigioso

Perché tutto sia chiaro, quel che segue
sono io, il mio diario, la mia autobiografia.
Io, cioè un personaggio, un'identità
fittizia: Rutebeuf, Malone, Prufrock
o quel che resta di Icio, nato
e vissuto sei anni al Cairo.

***

Ho un cervello meccanografico
verde, argenteo, mirabilmente minuzioso
e munitissimo, espandibile, ergonomico,
con prodigiosi allestimenti di piastrine,
moduli di memoria, dischi ottici,
diffusori acustici, un chip audio evoluto
a 478 piedini, un dissipatore
silenzioso, efficiente, progettato
per non stressare la madre.

Mi tasto il cranio per godere
gli innumerevoli impulsi sempre attivi,
le scosse, i tic, le belle vibrazioni degli slot.
Da quella lastra appesa al muro appare
una città operosa, o una colata di Pollock.
E quei fili di vetro ad alta trasparenza!

A Fictitious Identity and a Prodigious Brain

Just so that everything is clear, what follows
is I, my diary, my autobiography.
I—i.e., a personage, a fictitious
identity: Rutebeuf, Malone, Prufrock
or else what's left of Icio, who was born
and lived for six years at the Cairo.

***

I possess a data-processor of a brain,
green and silvery, admirably meticulous
and fully equipped, expandable, ergonomic,
prodigiously outfitted with integrated
circuits, memory modules, optic discs,
acoustic diffusers, an audio chip advanced
to 478 pins, and an efficient
and silent cooling fan designed so as not
to overstress the motherboard.

I touch my cranium to enjoy
the innumerable ever-active impulses,
tics, tremors, pleasant vibrations of the slots.
Through that pane hanging on the wall appears
an industrious city, or a flow of Pollock.
And those glass fibers of high transparency!

Ammetto un po' di confusione, di emozione,
ma ho controllato il processore di linguaggio
poi ho deciso di aggiornare il bios.

***

Ho appeso al gancio per la notte
una camicia di flanella e il golf
perché se mi alzo per pisciare
i brividi mi squassano e mi viene
da urlare o tossire e vomitare sbronza.
L'ho detto in giro agli amici
più giovani: impagliatemi
come una volpe o un gufo.
Non ho messo via niente
per il bel viaggio patetico.

***

Mi spossesso di me per dare campo,
dopo il distacco,
a infinite sequenze merceologiche.
La mia mistica è l'oggetto, l'acquisto,
il mio specchio di Narciso è la vetrina,
il mio cuore un immenso magazzino.

I admit to a bit of confusion, of emotion,
but I checked out the language processor
and then decided to upgrade the BIOS.

***

I hung a flannel shirt and the cardigan
on the hook because if I get out of bed
in the middle of the night to take a piss
I get the shivers and I start to feel
like yelling or coughing and drunken vomiting.
I've made the point to younger friends of mine
when I've been out and about: stuff me
with straw just like an owl or a fox.
I haven't put anything away
for the great pathetic journey.

***

I divest myself of me to open up space,
after the separation,
for an infinite parade of merchandise.
My mysticism is the thing, the purchase,
my mirror of Narcissus the display case,
my heart is an enormous warehouse.

L'atlante dell'anima

Pullula, e di continuo rigermina,
scaturisce e affiora dalle porosità
infinitesimali,
dalle frattaglie e dai frustoli,
dal macinato ai globuli
ai villi e microvilli e soprattutto
si scatena lì, si incrocia
si imbeve e si sparge,
indecifrabile materia,
dalle caverne e dai succhi e genera
sentimenti e visioni,
sentori, panico, euforia, rigurgiti
e figure della mente,
protocollo cangiante dell'anima.

**

Non ho voluto mai sapere il contenuto,
la trama, il meccanismo del giocattolo.
Neppure da bambino, indifferente
agli ingranaggi, a quello che c'è dentro.
Ma per fortuna non sono più
l'esangue fanciullo sparuto
e mi ha salvato l'egoismo.

**

The Atlas of the Soul

It pullulates and regerminates without ceasing,
gushes and surfaces from the infinitesimal
porosities,
from the guts and from the bits,
from the ground meal to the corpuscles
to the villi and microvilli and most of all
it runs wild there, it intersects
it saturates and disseminates,
indecipherable substance,
from cavities and juices and generates
sentiments and visions,
inklings, panic, euphoria, overflowings
and figures of the mind,
the prismatic protocol of the soul.

***

I never wanted to know about the design,
the works or the mechanics of a toy.
Even when I was a boy I didn't care
about the gears or what might be inside.
But luckily I'm not him anymore,
that pasty-faced and rawboned kid,
and my salvation has been selfishness.

***

Mauro aveva ancora
la sua faccia tirata,
la pelle liscia e il corpo stagno
dell'atleta. Fosse in tuta
o in pigiama da ospedale
mi ha indicato, al muro, un atlante
colorato. Pensavo che le cavità
fossero immensa
vacuità viscosa
e invece sono spugna o massa
polposa. Eppure tutto
così mirabile e perfetto,
sulla struttura fortemente vertebrata,
ma non di meno cruento, compresso
nella sua economia in crescita
vertiginosa, esponenziale.

***

Pelle o budello, comunque sia, non cambia.
Ogni soggetto, unico e irripetibile,
si ottiene solo in aree geografiche ben definite.
Nelle regioni più calde risultiamo più sapidi.
Nelle regioni più fredde siamo di norma dolci.

La qualità delle carni, se idonea,
presenta un colore uniforme rosso chiaro,
una consistenza soda e una superficie
al taglio non acquosa.

***

Mauro still possessed
the drawn face,
the smooth skin and the sturdy body of
an athlete. Whether in a sweatsuit
or a pair of hospital pajamas
he pointed out to me a colored atlas
on the wall. I thought the cavities
were immense
viscous vacuities
but what they really are is a sponge
or a pulpy mass. And yet
all so marvelous and perfect,
on a structure strongly vertebrate
but bloody nonetheless, compressed
in its economy in a vertiginous
exponential growth.

* * *

Skin or bowel, be that as it may, it doesn't change.
Every specimen, unique and unrepeatable,
is obtained only in well-defined geographical areas.
In warmer regions we turn out more savory.
In cooler regions we tend as a rule to be sweet.

The quality of the meat, when it's suitable,
presents an even, clear, red coloration,
a solid texture and a surface that's not
aqueous when it's cut.

* * *

Teo, col suo sorriso acutissimo e nero,
con i suoi occhi a taglio, mi diceva: « Eccolo qui
l'atlante dei tuoi desideri ».
L'ho aperto e ho visto i fotogrammi e le sedi
viscide e molli dell'inconscio.

Tra meraviglia e orrore
ho considerato secrezioni e sintesi,
i succhi e il conseguente impasto,
le contrazioni ondulatorie, l'attività di accumulo
verso ulteriori forme degradate . . .
e i plessi, regolatori di inibizioni e stimoli.

Di seguito i lobi rosso-bruni filtranti,
i dotti, i canalicoli e le lamine,
l'istmo e le isole di Langerhans, le micelle
dell'interfaccia grasso-acquoso,
giù giù fino ai processi
putrefattivi e di fermentazione.

« Tutta roba per i sacchi dell'umido » ho fatto,
« però il reale non è così cieco e fangoso ».
E mentre con le mani mi forbivo la bocca,
gli occhi dell'amico erano due fessure.

***

La sua figura già massiccia saliva,
volava in alto su una fune o un gancio.

Teo, with his dark and most penetrating smile,
with his eyes narrowed to cracks, said to me: "Look,
here is the atlas of your desires."
I opened it and I saw the stills and saw
the soft and slimy seats of the unconscious.

Between astonishment and disgust
I considered the secretions and synthesis,
the juices and the paste that they produced,
the wavelike contractions, the briskness of piling up
toward ever more degenerated forms . . .
and the plexuses, regulators of inhibitions and stimuli.

One after another the red-brown filtering lobes,
the ducts, the canaliculi, the laminae,
the isthmus and islands of Langerhans, the micelles
of the fatty-aqueous interface,
going way down to the processes
of putrefaction and of fermentation.

"All stuff for sacks of dampness," I remarked,
"but reality is not so blind and greasy."
And while I raised my hands and wiped my mouth,
my friend's eyes were a pair of narrow slits.

***

And his now enormous form was rising,
flying overhead on a rope or hook.

La pazienza degli affetti

Questa volta ho sognato
che ci siamo persi in due
nell'incubo nebbioso,
accogliente, della periferia.

Ma quest'inverno il bel vagone rosa
con i cuscini blu e le inquiete bestiole
ci porterà nel porto.

C'è uno strano chiarore nel tempo
e non sai mai qual è, nel sogno,
la tua vera casa.

**

Pentesilea

Dolce pasto mattutino ai cani
e miele sulla cappa di cucina
acacia millefiori tiglio.
Però che denti aguzzi
e che mastini che hai . . .
Ma come fai
a sbrodolarti così il mento
di un po' di petto e sangue
e di brandelli le mani?

**

The Patience of the Affections

This time I dreamed
that we're lost there,
separated, in the hazy
cozy suburban nightmare.

But this winter the beautiful pink railway car
with the blue cushions and the restless little creatures
will carry us to the harbor.

There is a peculiar radiance to time
and in the dream you never know which one
is your real home.

***

Penthesilea

A sweet meal in the morning to the dogs
and honey on the kitchen stove's exhaust fan
acacia millefiori linden tree.
And yet what rough and
pointed teeth you have . . .
But how do you
stain your chin like that
with a bit of brisket and blood
and your hands with scraps?

***

Il gatto siamese, come risulta dai manuali, ha un'affettività esigente, venata di una gelosia a volte aggressiva. Chiede il contatto fisico, ama accoccolarsi composto sulle gambe e tra le braccia del padrone, tanto è vero che Gigia miagola e mi si arrampica sui pantaloni, e si adagia volentieri, facendo fusa rumorose sulle spalle e sul collo.

Poi la osservo mentre con gli occhi semichiusi si acciambella sul divano, e si sistema meglio, rassicurata, e sbadiglia.

Ho cercato di penetrare il segreto dei suoi ritmi, delle sue ore di meditazione e stasi, di fame e vivo sentimento. Ho seguito così le sue abitudini, che sono poche ma esattissime: al mattino, per esempio, si deposita sulle mie gambe, giace sulla coperta.

Mi incanta la sua giornata, scandita, non so se con gioia o indifferenza, dalle solenni dormite, dal passeggio improvviso verso i croccantini, dai pasti furtivi o frugali, dallo strusciarsi per odore sugli spigoli, dal suo parlottare oscuro e petulante.

Fin quando, ceduta l'ambizione vana di educarla, sono rapidamente asceso al suo modello. Facile con il sonno, che mi concedo, sano e abbondante anche se il mio scenario onirico, temo, sia più scosceso e turbato del suo, che intuisco talvolta da impercettibili tremiti e ovattati ronfamenti.

Ho poi cercato di assecondarla nel linguaggio, imitandone a risposta gli urletti minimi e i dolci gorgoglii. Mi sono spinto ad assaggiare dalle ciotole le sue delizie secche per l'aperitivo . . .

Ma adesso puoi vederci entrambi al sole del terrazzo, sdraiati accanto a grattarci la schiena contro il pavimento, mentre agitiamo le nostre quattro zampe verso il cielo di questo sapido paesaggio animale.

***

The Siamese cat, as is pointed out in the guidebooks, has a demanding affectivity, tinged with a jealousy that is at times aggressive. It seeks physical contact, it loves to nestle calmly on its master's legs and in his arms, so much so that Gigia meows and climbs up on my pants, and lies down with pleasure, purring loudly on my shoulders and my neck.

Then I watch her as with her eyes half closed she curls up on the couch, arranges herself, reassured, and yawns.

I tried to penetrate the secret of her rhythms, of her hours of meditation and stasis, of hunger and vivid emotion. So I attended to her habits, which are few but most precise: in the morning, for instance, she settles on my legs, and lies on the blanket.

I'm enchanted by the progress of her day, articulated, I don't know whether with joy or indifference, by spells of solemn sleep, by a sudden promenade toward the kibble, by stealthy or sparing meals, by rubbing herself on corners because of a scent, by her insistent and mysterious muttering.

Until, having abandoned the vain desire to train her, I have rapidly raised myself to her example. Easy enough with sleep, which I indulge in soundly and copiously, even if my oneiric scenario, I fear, is more abrupt and agitated than hers, which I intuit sometimes by imperceptible tremors and muffled snoring.

Then I tried to accommodate myself to her linguistically, responsively imitating her tiny yowls and sweet gurgles. I went as far as sampling the dry delicacies of her bowl as an appetizer . . .

But now you can see us both in the sun on the terrace, lying close together scratching our backs on the floor, while we wave our four paws at the sky of this savory animal landscape.

***

Mi infilo nel portafogli del mio letto
come una carta d'identità scaduta.
Amo, del resto, questa mia fronte spaziosa
che giorno per giorno immagino e coltivo.

***

L'uomo che mangia da solo
seduto al bar e legge la Gazzetta
ghigna tra i baffi e il sugo
mentre passano in fila i giapponesi.
Si stira e stende un po', beato,
le gambe sotto il tavolo.
"Sono al *Cabaret Vert*
straniero e sospeso nella luce,
qui c'è il fiato sereno
di un'armonia leggera
senza colpa."
Soddisfatto e indolente,
dopo un ultimo sorso,
si alza e canticchia *Cielito Lindo*
e nella luce alta che declina lenta
sente un leggero brivido:
è l'inattesa gioia della solitudine.

***

Non so neanch'io, seduto a questo tavolo,
mentre accarezzo trasognato il calice
se è per salire leggerissimo nell'aria
o sprofondare nelle caverne, cupo,
se per il gusto, per il torpore o il sogno . . .

I slip into the wallet of my bed
like an identity card that's out of date.
Besides, I love this spacious brow of mine
that I picture every day and cultivate.

***

The man who's eating by himself
at the café and reading the *Gazette*
sneers between his mustache and the juice
while a row of Japanese go passing by.
Blissful, he spreads out a bit and stretches
his legs under the table.
"I'm at the *Cabaret Vert*
a foreigner suspended in the light,
here there's the tranquil breeze
of a weightless guilt-free
harmony."
Satisfied and listless,
after one final sip,
he gets to his feet and hums *Cielito Lindo*
and in the high light slowly on the wane
he senses a slight shiver:
it's the unexpected joy of solitude.

***

I don't know either, sitting at this table,
stroking the goblet, lost in a daydream,
if it's by the gentlest rising in the air
or sinking darkly into caverns,
or by the taste, the torpor or the dream . . .

So che va giù spedito
questo rosso che macchia
il bavaglino e l'anima,
questo rosso mostoso che va giù sul mento,
questo rosso bramato, giustamente lodato
in tutte le lingue del mondo.

Sbegascèmm, scudellèm, fèmm bandoria,
stramazzàmmoce in terra de traverso,
con un sorriso al re dell'universo.

***

L'amministratore mi svegliava inatteso,
prima del viaggio, fino a farmi affondare.
È stato così che li ho visti annidarsi
orribili in gruppi sociali
negli angoli dei muri, marroni che quasi volavano
come uccelli di Hitchcock, poltiglia schiacciata
nei buchi in cucina, tra i sacchetti e i rifiuti.
È stato così che ho visto le unghie
dei piedi ritorte, le unghie
cerchiate di nero e gialle di fumo,
le sedie spalmate di schifo, impiastrato
per terra, le cicche, le scarpe e i vestiti
a mucchi sul letto, sulle lenzuola fradice.

Attorno i vicini storpi che annusano,
sul portone il camion rosso dei pompieri
e le tue povere urla sulle scale,
mentre ti portano via seduta,
piccolo corpo dal viso stravolto, depresso,

I know it goes down fast,
this red that leaves a stain
on the bib and on the soul,
this musty red that dribbles down the chin,
this longed-for red, so justly celebrated
in all the languages of the world.

We booze, we guzzle, we go on a binge,
collapsing splayed out on the ground transverse,
with a smile for the king of the universe.

***

The administrator would wake me unexpectedly,
before the trip began, and make me go under.
And that was how I saw them horribly
lurking in social clusters
at the corners of the walls, chestnuts that practically flew
like Hitchcock's birds, pulp flattened into the holes
in the kitchen, between the bags and the garbage.
And that was how I saw the nails
of the twisted feet, the nails
ringed with black and yellow with smoke,
the chairs all coated with filth, smeared on
the floor, the cigarette butts, the shoes and clothes
all piled up on the bed, on the soaked sheets.

The crippled neighbors sniffing all around,
the bright red firetruck at the main door
and your wretched shrieking coming from the stairs,
you seated as they carry you away,
small body with a sad and frantic face,

che ogni tanto riesce a abbassarsi dolce
per dirmi: « Mi ricordo di lui,
così maschio e gentile,
mi ricordo di te, che volavi al laghetto
e alzavi le braccia, uccellino felice di vivere.
Io ti chiedo perdono, ma è andata così. »

***

Chi è quello che va lassù,
lento sulla cresta a mento basso,
sagoma ombrosa che si accende di sé?

managing now and then to gently subside
and tell me: "I remember him,
so manly and refined,
I remember you, who flew to the lake and raised
your arms, a little bird happy to be alive.
I beg your pardon, but that's how it went."

***

Who is that going by up there,
slowly over the crest with head bent low,
a shadowy shape that lights itself with itself?

da VITE PULVISCOLARI (2009)

from DUSTY LIVES (2009)

Il denaro e gli oggetti

a Sandro Martini

La memoria insiste
sul legno abraso e opaco
dove la mano, nel tempo,
briciola su briciola, minima, invisibile,
ha eroso d'affetto il suo colore, il rosso,
il rosso umano dell'attrezzo.
In queste fruste teche barocche,
resiste l'attrezzo antico, povero
come la mano attiva. Povero e enorme
come la macchina meccanica
nobile e astrusa, cieco ordigno
che ruota e lavora la piazza.
Le cose, vedi, si nutrono di noi, ci assorbono
nelle crepe e nei cunicoli
sfaldati del colore, nelle ditate
che macchiano un po' l'impugnatura,
la vernice. Ci assorbono, le cose,
nei pori pazienti. Ma oggi
di meno, sempre meno, perché
siamo altrove, schermati. Ricordi
il cordaio di Roma, il vasaio del Nilo?
L'oggetto, avvilito,
non ha più da noi il suo nome,
né senso di terra e di cuore.
Ci è accanto remoto. Così,
senza traccia né attrito, ci siamo
estraniati, ci siamo un po' persi
in questa identità pulviscolare.

Money and Things

to Sandro Martini

Memory insists
on opaque and abraded wood
where the hand, over time,
bit by bit, minute, invisible,
has eroded the sentiment from its color, the red,
the human red of the implement.
In these shabby baroque reliquaries,
the antique implement withstands, poor
as the active hand. Poor and enormous
as the admirable and abstruse
mechanical engine, blind device
that revolves and works the square.
Things, you see, feed on us, absorb us
in the fissures and the tunnels
with color flaking, in the fingermarks
that leave a bit of smudging on the handle,
the paint. They absorb us, things,
in their patient pores. But less
today, and always less, because
we're somewhere else, and shielded. Do you recall
the ropemaker of Rome, the potter of the Nile?
The object, dispirited,
no longer has its name among us,
or a sense of either earth or heart.
It's close at hand remote from us. And thus,
with neither trace nor friction, we
are cut off, we're a little lost
in this dusty identity.

***

Me ne restavo muto al tavolo osservando
le buste bianche e le monete, le scritte
come "Caro Pane". Aspettavo
la fine del gioco del sabato, mentre lui
era già lì pronto, nero nella veste, come neri
erano i suoi bei capelli e gli occhi.
Aspettavo i residui, quei pochi avanzi
per qualche figurina. E poi nei prati,
Masciadri, il fisarmonicista, l'amico
che oggi vorrei tanto avere, dietro lo sguardo
franco sul testone e gli occhialini
apriva il borsellino sorridendo e mi diceva
« Potrei comprarmi il mondo intero ».

***

Il nano ragioniere dai capelli grigi,
coi denti di coniglio e le calzette bianche,
sotto i calzoni grigi alla caviglia,
si tirava come un pupazzo alla lavagna
disegnando strane forme di T:
i mastrini, diceva, del dare e dell'avere;
e a me sembrava osceno, vergognoso,
parlare di teoria dei soldi a scuola.

***

***

I stayed there silent at the table taking
note of the white envelopes and coins,
inscriptions like "Expensive Bread." I was waiting
for Saturday's game to be over, while he was already
there and ready, black inside his clothes,
that were as black as his beautiful hair and eyes.
I was waiting for the leftovers, those few scraps
for some picture cards. And then out in the fields,
Masciardi, the accordionist, the friend
I'd like so much to have today, behind
the frank gaze on his large head and his glasses
opened his coin purse with a smile and told me
"I could buy myself the whole wide world."

***

The runt of an accountant with gray hair,
with teeth just like a rabbit's and white socks
under gray pants that reached down to his ankles,
pulled himself up to the blackboard like a puppet
drawing strange designs in the shape of a T:
the little ledgers, he said, of debit and credit,
and to me it seemed shameful and obscene to be
talking in school about monetary theory.

***

Gli oggetti sono cambiati, sono cambiato io.
Erano fatti per resistere, durare anche oltre noi;
costavano fatica, sangue, soldi,
erano carta assorbente opaca
che tramandava affetti e memorie.
Oggi sono lisci, lucenti, spettacolari
mucchi immensi di opulenza iniqua,
impermeabili, scivolano via
di mano, viscidi, io stesso
nel processo del tempo destinato
a questo oceano sgargiante di immondizia.

***

Cuore e immondizia

Se pure il cuore
è ancora un immenso magazzino,
le cose ormai sono altre cose:
mutate, luccicanti e più che mai
fungibili.
Non più porose, affabili e il passo
dalla vetrina alla montagna
enorme, epica della ruera,
è diventato minimo, una freccia
liberatoria verso il più vario,
indifferenziato, eroico
spettacolo spettacolare
che ci sommerge e esalta.

***

Things have changed around me, and I've changed.
They were made to withstand, and to outlast us;
they cost labor, they cost blood and money,
they were a kind of opaque blotting paper
that handed down emotions and memories.
Today they're shiny, smooth, spectacular
immense heaps of iniquitous opulence.
Impermeable, they slip away
through the hands, slimy, I myself
destined in the course of time to be
tossed into this gaudy ocean of garbage.

***

Heart and Garbage

Even if the heart
is still an enormous warehouse,
things are now other things:
altered, glistening, and more than ever
fungible.
No longer porous and affable and the step
from the window to the enormous
mountain, an epic of rubbish,
has become minimal, a liberating
signpost toward the most varied,
undifferentiated, heroic,
spectacular spectacle
that overwhelms and exalts us.

***

Nel crepuscolo mattone
lungo la torre di mattoni
altissima salivano uno
e poi l'altro gli operai
tra il ponte e le teste
chine sull'opera in un quadro
piatto e virtuale che ci sottrae
realtà, storia, lavoro,
umana conoscenza. Così
come piatta, bidimensionale
è la scena spossessata
di questa nostra esperienza
ridotta a una lamina
a una pellicola sottile.

In the brick-red twilight
along the towering brick
tower they climbed one
and then the other one workers
between the bridge and the heads
bent over their work in a flat
and virtual picture that extracts
reality, history, labor,
human awareness. Flat as
that, as two-dimensional,
is the dispossessed scene
of this experience of ours
reduced to a sheet
to a thin film.

La traversata

Arrivo al porto con l'ansia
e la gioia dell'avventura.
È stato difficile. Voglio dire venir fuori
per vivere. Star dentro
per non morire, e dire:
ventre, acqua, tetto, morbido
cuore, letto.

***

Nell'attesa, per quei pochi minuti
mi accomodo sereno e vedo
come un film, per me, la sospensione,
il giorno che agisce fresco e scorre
nei gesti degli uomini.

Sento le cose ruvide
addosso, mie. Le cose
sporche e piene. Così
ci sono dentro. Anch'io.

Sarà la polvere nel vento
leggero, la barca sudicia e il rampone,
la cassetta, il guanto del pescatore,
le macchie d'olio, le cicche,
i saluti scomposti e le risate,
l'odore del cuoio che mi piace.

***

The Crossing

I arrive at the port with the anxiety
and the joy of the adventure.
It's been hard. I mean, coming outside
to live. Staying inside
to not die, and saying:
belly, water, roof, soft
heart, bed.

***

In the meantime, for those few minutes
I settle down peacefully and see
like a movie, for me, the suspension,
the day that proceeds coolly and flows
in the deeds of men.

I sense rough things
nearby, mine. Things
dirty and solid. Just so
are they inside us. Even me.

There'll be dust in the gentle
wind, the mucky boat and the harpoon,
the chest, the fisherman's rubber glove,
the oil stains, the cigarette butts,
the coarse greetings and bursts of laughter,
the leather smell I love.

***

L'insegnamento è sempre uguale:
succhiare questa sola radice di terra
con ansia, sfiorare questa macchia di morchia.
Se no perdiamo vita, presente e conoscenza.
Perdiamo conoscenza. L'incontro
dev'essere in attrito
diretto e fisico fino a farsi
abrasivo:
ruvido il mondo,
l'esperienza
abrasiva.
Far fruttare anche il minimo gesto.

***

È tutto pieno nel suo passaggio,
vivo. Come l'aurora, il vento
o questo mediocre paesaggio
carico di memoria, affetti,
e quest'angoscia distratta.

***

Guardo con attenzione, indugio
diligente e curioso. Non so.
Guardo il furgone azzurro, il risalto
granuloso di ruggine che mangia
materia, che mangia la materia.
L'autista che carica i bagagli,
le unghie cerchiate di nero,
le dita nere, sorridente,
la cicca tra le labbra, la camicia
appiccicata alla schiena.

The lesson is always the same:
to suck upon this one root of the earth
anxiously, to skim over this sludge stain.
If not we lose life, present and awareness.
We lose awareness. The encounter
must be in direct
and physical friction till it turns
abrasive:
the world rough,
experience
abrasive.
So that even the least act may be productive.

***

All is full in its passage,
alive. Like the dawn, the wind
or this mediocre landscape
loaded with memory, feelings,
and this absent-minded anguish.

***

I look attentively, I linger
conscientious and curious. I don't know.
I look at the light blue van, the grainy
prominence of the rust that eats
matter, that eats the matter.
The driver loading the baggage,
nails ringed with black,
black fingers, smiling,
cigarette between his lips, shirt
sticking to his back.

Max e il camionista che al volo
si passano le casse pesantissime:
da fracassare i muscoli, i muscoli
che invece tengono.

***

La traversata, così attesa. Il battello
screpolato, mezz'ora di avventura. Mi sposto,
guardo in alto la casa anche per me
intonacata di luce.
Scavalco la merce, le valigie
e l'operaio che si guarda le mani.
Ha toccato la catena e ha le dita
tutte macchiate di morchia.

***

Seduto in fondo, rido per l'acqua
che arriva a schizzi sui sedili
sverniciati. Ho visto il volto terreo
dell'oste, il grande corpo
smangiato e d'improvviso, con un brivido,
il cranio rasato della dolce postina. Parlottavo,
leggero. Ma quando ho mosso lo sguardo
verso l'orizzonte
è sceso un cupo silenzio
e mi ha assorbito. *Desideroso
di luce e terra l'orizzonte è una lama,
uno specchio che mi cancella.*

***

Max and the driver passing one another
the heaviest crates on the fly:
enough to shred muscles, the muscles
that nonetheless hold.

***

The crossing, waited for like that. The cracked
boat, a half hour's adventure. I move around,
up above I see the house that looks to me
to be plastered with light.
I step over the packages, the valises
and the workman who's looking at his hands.
He touched the chain and now his fingers are
all stained with sludge.

***

Seated astern, I laugh to see the water
come lapping up to splash the seats that have
been stripped of varnish. I saw the innkeeper's
doughy face, the great
gnawed body and suddenly, with a shudder,
the shaved skull of the sweet postwoman. I chatted,
lightly. But when I shifted my glance
toward the horizon
a dark silence descended
and absorbed me. *Desirous*
of light and earth the horizon is a blade,
a mirror that erases me.

***

Oppure una linea sottile,
immaginaria, che si intreccia a cappio,
orlo di un precipizio, un Maelström,
che chissà cosa inghiotte e annulla,
divora eternamente; sul disco piatto
della terra, sotto il sole che va.
Una sabbia mobile o un invisibile
immenso borro
di un astro immenso collassato.

***

Mi venivano in mente,
mentre guardavo gli amici malati,
certe strane idee.
Dio, anima: parole,
concetti remotissimi, inservibili,
bolle svuotate, strutture
di pensiero arcaico.

***

Il marinaio scende nella botola
con uno straccio, fischiettando,
e dal fondo si alza subito un rumore
assordante di macchina. Poi ricompare,
si aggiusta il berretto sulla fronte
e guarda l'orizzonte, indifferente.
Sa già che presto si rivedrà il paese.

Or an imaginary
thin line instead, that braids into a slipknot,
the very edge of a precipice, a Maelström,
and who knows what it swallows and annuls,
devours eternally; on the flat disk
of the earth, under the passing sun.
A quicksand or an invisible
immense gully
of an immense collapsed star.

***

There came into my mind,
while I was looking at my ailing friends,
certain strange ideas.
God, soul: words,
the most remote and unusable of concepts,
empty bubbles, structures
of archaic thought.

***

The sailor goes down the hatch
with a rag in his hand, whistling,
and from below comes a sudden deafening roar
of machinery. Then he reappears, adjusts
his cap on his brow and looks indifferently
at the horizon. Now he already knows
that soon we'll be seeing land once more.

Ho sentito la mia voce che diceva:
« Tutto è materia, c'è un vorticare
di materia. Fuori, dentro di noi,
nel cosmo, in questo sasso
che sto gettando in mare, in quello
che tu chiami il vuoto, o che tu chiami
lo spazio. Aggregazioni varie di materia
orribili e mirabili. Campi e forze,
vibrazioni che creano
materia ».

***

Evapora poi lento, nel tempo
che non sappiamo, lento, in un crescendo
di luminosità, l'enorme
caverna materia, spaziale.
Inarrestabile
diventa allora lieve, evanescente
e il suo orizzonte
al confine estremo delle cose,
degli eventi, sembra dissolversi
e svanire
lasciandosi alle spalle il nulla.

Ma che cos'è
il nulla?

***

I heard my voice and it was saying this:
"Everything is matter, there's a whirling
of matter. Outside us, inside us,
in the cosmos, in this rock
I'm throwing in the sea, in what
you call the void, or in what you call
space. Varied aggregations, horrible
and wonderful, of matter. Fields and forces,
vibrations that engender
matter."

**

Then it evaporates slowly, in a time
that we don't know, slowly, in a crescendo
of luminosity, the enormous
spatial cavern of matter.
Unstoppable
then it turns mild, evanescent,
and its horizon
at the extreme limit of things,
of events, seems to dissolve
and vanish
leaving nothing behind.

But what is it,
this nothing?

**

Allora ho pensato a te,
che mi chiamavi e alzando
quel poco lo sguardo ho osservato
prima indistinta, come una suggestione,
infine quasi chiara, una forma
avanzare, oscillare. Come una nave,
o di sicuro una nave
che rompeva l'orizzonte arrivando
in una strana, confusa evanescenza.
Come un messaggio sbucava, come
un'informazione viva
o superstite, integra,
emersa da un nero immenso tutto.

***

Infatti, sulla superficie vasta del deserto
d'ebano galleggiavano avanzi, rottami
rigettati dall'abbraccio del vortice, sottratti
al precipizio eterno.

***

Restava poco, pochissimo,
prima di mettere a terra il piede.
Sentivo il cibo covare attivo dentro,
caldo come un'eco di sapore
di calmo conforto silenzioso.
Il corpo-cibo della madre che ti scalda.
Pensavo anch'io: il grembo è tutto.

***

And then I thought of you,
who called to me, and lifting
my line of vision just a bit I saw
indistinct at first, like a suggestion,
then finally almost clear, a form
advancing, fluctuating. Like a ship,
or certainly a ship
that broke up the horizon, coming closer
in a peculiar, blurry evanescence.
Coming forward like a message, like
a live piece of information
or a survivor, intact,
it emerged from an immense black everything.

***

In fact, upon the ebony desert's vast
surface there was wreckage floating, scraps
rejected from the whirlpool's embrace, delivered
from the eternal precipice.

***

There was little, very little that remained
before putting a foot down on the ground.
I felt the food actively incubating
inside me, warm like the echo of a taste
of calm silent comfort.
The body-food of the mother that makes you warm.
I thought this too: the womb is everything.

***

Ecco le cose che ancora
sanno di noi, il semplice
che come nostro vive
nella mano e nel gesto,
negli occhi e nel cuore.
Le cose felici, perché nostre,
perché di noi ricolme.

Pierre vide il soldato,
l'ometto nei suoi gesti tondi,
accurati, sciogliersi le cordicelle
della gamba, appendere a un uncino
le scarpe, mettersi a posto gli abiti
che odoravano di lui.
Tutto il male, pensava, non viene
dalla mancanza delle cose,
ma dal loro superfluo.

***

Perché l'eccesso — dico io — distrae,
rende discreto, occasionale,
il tuo attrito vivo con le cose
e ti sottrae, così, vita, valore.

***

Ho chiuso in tasca il temperino
come inchiodando la freccia del tempo.
Sono qui, nel presente ablativo,
mio

Here are the things that still
know us, the plain and simple
that live, like what is ours,
in the hand and in the act,
in the eyes and in the heart.
Happy things, because they're ours,
because they're filled with us.

Pierre watched the soldier,
the little man in his precise and accurate
actions, undo the cords that were wrapped
around his legs, and hang up his shoes
on a hook, and put away his clothes
that smelled of him.
All the evil, he was thinking, comes
not from the lack of things,
but from their abundance.

***

Because the excess is—I say—distracting,
it takes your live friction with things
and makes it occasional and discreet,
thus subtracting life and value from you.

***

I closed the penknife in
my pocket as if nailing the arrow of time.
Here I am, in the ablative present,
my own

e mettendo già il piede sul suolo
mi fingo a me stesso più goffo
per darmi certezza del felice attrito
col mondo, con la materia
che mi accoglie e accarezza.
Che dolcemente mi azzera.

and now as I put my foot down on the soil
I pretend to myself I'm clumsier than I am
to give me the assurance of happy friction
with the world, with the matter
that accepts me and caresses me.
That gently resets me to zero.

Notes to the Poems

THE HOUSE, THE OUTSIDERS, THE NEAR RELATIONS

Fausto Coppi (1919–1960; see notes to "Glenn's Last Journey," below) and Gino Bartali (1914–2000) were Italian cyclists. Oscar Carboni (1914–1993) was an Italian popular singer who performed frequently on the radio.

PERSONAL BOOKLET

The term *libretto personale* refers to a booklet documenting the records of an individual student, worker, or member of the military.

THE PRINCIPLE

The epigraph ("O my my greatest good, dear body, I have only you!") is from "Fragments du Narcisse" in *Charmes* (1922) by French poet Paul Valéry (1871–1945).

FRESIA

This poem was written in 1980 and added to the 1994 republication of *Il disperso*. Cucchi has said that it is named for an early twentieth-century Italian soccer player. The reference might be to either Attilio Fresia (1891–1923) or Vincenzo Fresia (1888–1946).

MISTRESS OF THE GAME

Il Fiore is a medieval sequence of 232 sonnets that some have attributed to Dante, though many scholars reject the attribution. The epigraph is the last line of its sonnet, in which a woman advises her daughter not to put her heart in any one place, along with other advice that, if followed, will enable her to be "mistress of the game."

Botescià was Ottavio Bottecchia (1894–1927), an Italian cyclist, the winner of two Tours de France. On the morning of June 3, 1927, he was found unconscious by the side of a road near his home with a fractured skull and several broken bones, with his undamaged bicycle nearby; he died eleven days later. The circumstances of his death have never been satisfactorily explained.

IN MY HAPPY YEAR

The first epigraph ("The black point where I was, in the pale immensity of the sands, how could I wish him evil?") is from Samuel Beckett's *Molloy* (1947). The second ("and that death may find me planting my cabbages") is from Book I, Chapter 20, of the *Essais* (1580) of Michel de Montaigne (1533–1592).

MORNING SLEEP

The House by the Sea

The Brise Marine (French for *sea breeze*) is a hotel in Saint-Jean-Cap-Ferrat in southeastern France.

The Balanced Guest

The details in the first stanza are drawn from a stained glass window by Marc Chagall and from his painting *Le Poète allongé* (*The Poet Reclining*, 1915). The second stanza describes Diego Velázquez's painting *Las Meninas* (*The Maids of Honor*, 1656).

'53

"'[T]he Kamikaze, / Nacka, the man without a country, Poison': soccer players of that period (Ghezzi, Skoglund, Nyers, Lorenzi)" (M.C.).

Shop Window

Lambrate and Niguarda are districts of Milan.

Gorée

The island of Gorée is a district of Dakar, Senegal. Mozia is a small island near Marsala in northwest Sicily.

Letters of Carlo Michelstaedter

Carlo Michelstaedter (1883–1910) was an Italian philosopher and poet. He was very close to his mother, with whom he exchanged a series of letters during a separation shortly before his death. He had just completed his doctoral thesis after long and intense effort, when, on October 17, 1910, his mother's birthday, he shot himself after a violent quarrel with her.

AT THE CAIRO

"In the sequence 'At the Cairo' appear the names of Milanese buildings no longer standing: the Cairo and the Portascia. The Polveriera on the Corso Buenos Aires is, however, still there. The 'Schola,' the Confraternity of Prayer and Death, was based in the Church of Saint Gregory by the plague cemetery, outside the leper hospital. 'The consul general at Bogotà' is an affectionately ironic reference to Dossi" (M.C.).

Count Carlo Dossi (1849–1910) was an Italian writer and diplomat. Zenevredo, a small town in Lombardy, was his birthplace.

The Milan–San Remo bicycle race is held annually on March 19, at the beginning of spring.

La Società Italiana Smeriglio manufactured abrasives and ceramics. Bovisa is an industrial district in Milan. Martesana is a region northeast of Milan; a canal of that name flows into the city.

RUTEBEUF

"Playing on his name and on himself Rutebeuf writes: 'Rutebeuf qui est dit de "rude" et de "bœuf."'" I have appropriated and translated a few other lines from the great French poet, such as 'All that will happen has already happened'" (M.C.). Rutebeuf (which may or may not have been his actual name) was a Parisian, probably of humble origins. He was the author of elegies, satires, narrative poems, and fabliaux.

"The poet Jean Bodel of Arras, who was afflicted with leprosy, lived from the second half of the 1100s to about 1210. He couldn't therefore really have been a 'friend' of Rutebeuf (who was active from around 1250 to 1280), who was instead a contemporary of another poet of Arras, Baude Fastoul, also a leper" (M.C.).

"'He's wearing a shirt that reaches all the way': the figure to whom I refer illustrates the word 'idiocy' in the *Dizionario di cognizioni utili* ([*Dictionary of Useful Knowledge*], vol. III, Utet, Turin, 1924). The caption says only: 'A cretin'" (M.C.).

"'Genestas': character in Balzac's *Le médecin de campagne* [*The Country Doctor*, 1833]. This novel speaks of cretins in Alpine valleys, and their appearance as the last idols of other inhabitants of those places" (M.C.).

"'Finding myself . . .': In the first chapter of the *Storia della Colonna Infame* we read: 'On the morning of June 21, 1630, toward half past four, a silly gossip named Caterina Rosa, finding herself, by an unlucky chance, at a window of an overpass . . .'" (M.C.). *Storia della Colonna Infame* (*History of the Column of Infamy*, 1842), is a work by Alessandro Manzoni (1785–1873), published as an appendix to the revised edition of his great novel *I promessi sposi* (*The Betrothed*, 1827). It discusses the arrest, torture, and in some cases execution of a number of people who were accused of spreading the plague in Milan in 1630 by smearing contagious substances on walls and in other public places. The passage that Cucchi cites is actually the very beginning of the text.

"'Rosa['s engravings]': Salvator Rosa" (M.C.). Rosa (1615–1673) was an Italian Baroque painter.

ISLAND FOREST

The first piece in this sequence is a revised version of the earlier poem entitled "The House by the Sea."

SPIDERWEB

"The title of this section is from Enrico Della Torre" (M.C.). Della Torre (b. 1931) is an Italian painter and illustrator. *Ragna* is the title of a pastel drawing of his.

GLENN'S LAST JOURNEY

Lake Garda, Italy's largest lake, lies between Milan and Venice. The Ortler is a peak in the Eastern Alps, in northeastern Italy.

Mount Prato is in the northern Apennines, in the province of Lucca.

Olympia is a Milanese firm that manufactures parts and accessories for motorcycles and motorbikes.

French cyclist Maurice Archambaud (1906–1955) set the world one-hour record at the Vigorelli velodrome in Milan on November 3, 1937. His record was broken at Vigorelli on November 7, 1942, by Italian cyclist Fausto Coppi (1919–1960); Coppi was captured by the British in North Africa in April 1943 and held prisoner for the duration of the war. The Allied bombardment of Milan, which occurred throughout the war, was especially intense in 1942 and 1943.

"I arrived like a bleeding sack": "from the (revised) account of Giuseppe Bestetti in *Fronte russo: c'ero anch'io* [*Russian Front: I Was There*], edited by Giulio Bedeschi (Milan: Mursia, 1983)" (M.C.).

Bersaglieri are elite Italian light infantry, trained as marksmen. The Bug river flows through Poland, Belarus, and Ukraine. "Katyusha" (diminutive of *Yekaterina*) is a World War II-era Russian song, for which a rocket launcher was named. Dniepropetrovsk, formerly Yekaterinoslav, is a city in Ukraine, on the Dniepper River. An *izba* is a kind of rural Russian house made of logs.

"In the blinding landscape": "also from an account (by Luigi Salvanelli) in the Bedeschi book" (M.C.).

"*À qui ai-je . . .*": "from Balzac's *Colonel Chabert*" (M.C.). The passage reads: "To whom do I have the honor of speaking?" "Colonel Chabert." "Who?" "The one who died at Eylau." About a decade after the Battle of Eylau (1807) between Napoleon's army and the Russians, in which he was believed to have been killed, Col. Chabert (here introducing himself to his lawyer) returns to Paris to find his wife remarried and his fortune gone.

Lecco is a city in Lombardy about thirty miles north of Milan.

"From the Cairo to Loreto": "The Cairo (see the sequence 'At the Cairo,' above) was a balconied apartment building on the Corso Buenos Aires in Milan, torn down in the early 1970s. 'Loreto' is the Piazzale Loreto" (M.C.). The Piazzale Loreto is the large public square where the bodies of Mussolini, his mistress Clara Petacci, and several others were hung upside down from a gas station roof on April 29, 1945, after having been shot and killed the day before.

"Amanda Binet": "she is '*la demoiselle du comptoir*' of the grand café in Besançon in Stendahl's *Le Rouge et le Noir* [*The Red and the Black*, 1830]" (M.C.). Dispatched to a seminary in Besançon, the young Julian Sorel flirts with the beautiful "girl behind the counter"; though she is coquettishly responsive, the end of the incident leaves him feeling awkward and powerless.

Inverigo is a municipality in Lombardy, near the Swiss border.

Innocenti was an Italian manufacturer of automobiles and motor scooters from 1920 to 1996.

"[T]he miracle" is a term often applied to a period of sustained economic growth in Italy in the 1950s and early 1960s.

"*He sensed them . . .*": "from Federigo Tozzi's *Tre Croci* [*Three Crosses*, 1920]" (M.C.). Tozzi (1883–1920) wrote three novels and a number of short stories before his early death from pneumonia. Cucchi paraphrases a passage describing the deranged state of mind of Giulio Gambi—whose forgery of several financial instruments in an attempt to save his family's failing book-store has just been exposed—immediately before his suicide.

"*Alleluia: Exultabuntur*": The *Exultabuntur* ("They will exult") is the Gregorian-chant alleluia for All Saints' Day, November 1.

MALONE DOESN'T DIE

"The reference is, of course, to the character in Beckett's novel *Malone meurt* [*Malone Dies*, 1951]" (M.C.).

The story of Emmaus, with the appearance and subsequent vanishing of the risen Christ, is told in the Gospel of Luke, 24:13-35.

THE ATLAS OF THE SOUL

"*Mauro*: is the poet Mauro Maconi, my close friend, who died prematurely in 2001" (M.C.).

"*Teo*: the poet and painter Teo Bragagna, to whom I dedicate this poem" (M.C.).

THE PATIENCE OF THE AFFECTIONS

"'We booze . . . on a binge': a line by Carlo Porta, from *Brindes de Meneghin all'Ostaria* [*Meneghin's Toast at the Tavern*, 1810]. The following line is from Belli (*Er vino novo* [*The New Wine*])" (M.C.).

Carlo Porta (1775–1821) was the preeminent Milanese dialect poet. Giuseppe Gioachino Belli (1791–1863), one of Italy's greatest poets, wrote 2279 sonnets in the Romanesco dialect.

MONEY AND THINGS

"'[T]he ropemaker of Rome, the potter of the Nile': from the ninth of Rilke's *Duino Elegies*" (M.C.).

"*Expensive Bread*: wording that appeared on pay envelopes" (M.C.).

THE CROSSING

"Recurring here, through connection or correspondence, are elements of Poe's celebrated tale 'A Descent into the Maelström' and of suggestions drawn from texts on astrophysics such as Monica Colpi's *Buchi neri evanescenti, Stephen Hawking e la scommessa perduta* ([*Evanescent Black Holes: Stephen Hawking and the Lost Wager*], Rome: Nottetempo, 2005)" (M.C.).

"'plastered with light': from Attilio Bertolucci's *Verso le sorgenti del Cinghio* [*Toward the Sources of the Cinghio*, 1993]" (M.C.). Bertolucci (1911–2000), author of several prize-winning volumes of poetry, was the father of the film director Bernardo Bertolucci.

"*Pierre*: from *War and Peace*" (M.C.).

Acknowledgments

Thanks are due to Arnoldo Mondadori Editore, for permission to reproduce the Italian text, and to the editors of the following journals, in which some of these translations first appeared: *Café Review*: "Island Forest"; *Chelsea*: "Court of Miracles," "Fresia," "with a mouth sweet," "Couch," "'53," and "Poetry of the Source"; *Journal of Italian Translation*: "Letter and Prayer," "Shop Window," "Gorée," "Letters of Carlo Michelstaedter," and "The Atlas of the Soul"; *Poetry*: "The Lump in the Throat."

This translation includes the complete text of *L'ultimo viaggio di Glenn* and substantial selections from each of Cucchi's other books and booklets, with the exception of *La luce del distacco* (1990), a book-length monodrama republished in an expanded edition as *Jeanne d'Arc e il suo doppio* (2008); my translation of this work was published by Gradiva in 2011 as *Jeanne d'Arc and Her Double*. My text for Cucchi's first six collections is his *Poesie 1965–2000*, in which certain poems have been revised since their original publication. The selections from *Per un secondo o un secolo* and *Vite pulviscolari* have been taken from their original editions.

I am grateful to a number of friends and colleagues for their assistance: to Alfredo de Palchi, who first suggested that I undertake this project and who supported it through the stages of its completion; to Luigi Fontanella, who provided me with a copy of the otherwise unobtainable *Per un secondo o un secolo* and who shed welcome light on several difficult passages throughout the work; to Luigi Bonaffini, who offered a number of valuable suggestions and corrections to the translation; to Ned Condini, who carefully read and amended both the Italian and English texts; to Lisa Cicchetti, for her elegant design of the book, both inside and out; to Areta Buk, for her flawless typesetting through several rounds of corrections; and to Maurizio Cucchi, for his poetry and his patience.

About the Author

MAURIZIO CUCCHI was born on September 20, 1945, in Milan, where he continues to live. His first seven volumes of poetry—from *Il disperso* (1976) to *L'ultimo viaggio di Glenn* (1999)—are collected in *Poesie 1965–2000* (2001), which has been followed by *Per un secondo o un secolo* (2003), *Jeanne d'Arc e il suo doppio* (2008), and *Vite pulviscolari* (2009). He has published three novels, *Il male è nelle cose* (2005), *La maschera ritratto* (2011), and *L'indifferenza del'assassino* (2012). His other prose works are *La traversata di Milano* (2007), an evocative walking tour of his native city, and *Cronache di poesia del Novecento* (2010), a collection of essays and articles. A former editor of the monthly magazine *Poesia*, he is the editor of *Dizionario della poesia italiana* (1983; 1990) and the co-editor (with Stefano Giovanardi) of the anthology *Poeti italiani del secondo Novecento* (1996; 2004) in the prestigious Meridiani series. He has also translated a number of authors into Italian, including Stendahl, Flaubert, Lamartine, Villiers de l'Isle-Adam, Mallarmé, Prévert, and Valéry.

About the Translator

MICHAEL PALMA was born on September 21, 1945. His poetry collections are *The Egg Shape*, *Antibodies*, *A Fortune in Gold*, and *Begin in Gladness*, and an Internet chapbook, *The Ghost of Congress Street: Selected Poems*, on The New Formalist Press website. His twelve previous translations of modern Italian poets include prize-winning volumes of Guido Gozzano and Diego Valeri with Princeton University Press, as well as Cucchi's monodrama *Jeanne d'Arc and Her Double* (Gradiva, 2011). His fully rhymed translation of Dante's *Inferno* was published by Norton in 2002 and reissued as a Norton Critical Edition in 2007.